The Sociology of
Labour Markets

STUDIES IN SOCIOLOGY

Series Editor: Professor W. M. Williams, University College of Swansea

The aim of this series is to provide essential surveys of key concepts in sociology. Each book reviews the present state of the art, identifies major issues and problems, and examines possible solutions and future avenues of research.

Other titles in the series include:

Friendship: Developing a Sociological Perspective
Graham Allan, University of Southampton

Imagine No Possessions: Towards a Sociology of Poverty
Brian K. Taylor, Roehampton Institute, London

Urban Sociology: Society, Locality and Human Nature
Peter Dickens, University of Sussex

Sociology and Development: Theories, Policies and Practices
David Hulme, University of Manchester and Mark M. Turner, Australian National University.

The Sociology of Labour Markets

RALPH FEVRE
University College of Swansea

HARVESTER
WHEATSHEAF

New York London Toronto Sydney Tokyo Singapore

First published 1992 by
Harvester Wheatsheaf
66 Wood Lane End, Hemel Hempstead,
Hertfordshire, HP2 4RG
A division of
Simon & Schuster International Group

Typeset in 10/12 pt Linotron Sabon
by Columns Design & Production Services Ltd

Printed and bound in Great Britain by
Billing and Sons Ltd, Worcester

British Library Cataloguing in Publication Data

Fevre, Ralph
 The sociology of labour markets.
 – (Studies in sociology)
 I. Title II. Series
 331.12

 ISBN 0–7450–0828–3
 ISBN 0–7450–0829–1 pbk

1 2 3 4 5   96 95 94 93 92

CONTENTS

PREFACE

This is a book about how people get jobs (or not) and employers get workers (or not). In other words, it is a book about something that matters to almost everyone. Most of us are involved in labour markets several times in our lives, and some of us are involved a great many more times than this. What happens there is very important for all of us: it affects our incomes, our happiness and health, even our life expectancies.

I have to thank Chris Harris for the original suggestion that I write this book, and Bill Williams – the series editor – and Clare Grist – the commissioning editor at Harvester Wheatsheaf – for making it a reality. As far as the content of the book is concerned, I should thank a great many people for their comments and criticisms but especially my anonymous referees, together with David Jones, Maureen Fevre, and my students past and present in the University of Wales (at both Bangor and Swansea).

None of the people mentioned above are responsible for any mistakes or omissions in what follows and it is to these that I now turn. This book attempts to systematise sociologists' observations about labour markets. Its first task is, therefore, to define the field for this relatively new subject area of sociology. In the process there may well have been some oversimplification, and the omission of some important items in the literature has been unavoidable.

This book summarises the sociology that has gone into the study of labour markets, but it is not a survey of the sociological literature, and it does not present a static picture which short-circuits the possibility of future development in the field. The final chapter, in particular, is concerned with future improvements in our knowledge of the workings of labour markets. Readers will judge the book according to their own criteria, but if they do not find it boring, and find some of it thought-provoking, then I will have achieved my aim in writing it.

Ralph Fevre
Swansea
April 1991

1

LABOUR MARKETS AND SOCIOLOGY

INTRODUCTION

If you have ever looked for a job, or ever intend to look for one, then you know something about the way a labour market works. You also know how important the labour market can be; you know that what happens to you when you enter the market can shape your whole life. If you do not know these things you are exceptional: over the last two or three centuries, more and more people have come to depend on labour markets. Industrialisation and the development of capitalism have put an ever-increasing proportion of the world's population in the role of job-seekers at some point in their lives.

In the last years of the twentieth century, the increasing influence of labour markets is most remarkable in those countries with short histories of sustained industrialisation or capitalist development. For example, there is little that is more dramatic (and, sometimes, tragic) than mass migrations in underdeveloped countries which are in part caused by the development of labour markets. Every third world city owes much of its cramped living conditions, its shanty towns, and its street beggars to the migration of people from rural areas to the city in an often vain search for work.

For the most part, however, this book is not concerned with the pains endured by societies in which labour markets are under-developed, but with things that the majority of readers will find more familiar – the labour markets of their own, established

1

industrial societies. It is many years since any of the cities of North America and Europe grew at anything like the rate of Mexico City, Guadalajara or Caracas, but there have been more recent dramas of a different kind in the established industrial societies[1]. The following pages will briefly demonstrate that labour markets in all of these societies bear little resemblance to the markets which existed twenty or thirty years ago. Labour market conditions are very different, and so are the ways in which markets are organised and regulated, for example by governments. Furthermore, it is not only the markets that have changed out of all recognition, but also the ways in which we think, speak and write about labour markets.

Let us begin by examining some significant changes in labour market conditions. But readers should note at the outset that, while labour markets in all established industrial societies have undergone enormous changes in recent years, these changes have not always been of the same type or direction in each of these societies. We therefore start with a qualification: *in general* the number of people using labour markets in these societies has increased, and, *in general*, this increase has not resulted from indigenous population growth (indeed, ageing populations in some countries, such as the United Kingdom, suggest quite the reverse, at least in the medium term). Rather, the most important influences have been international labour migrations and increases in the proportion of the population which seeks paid work (an increase in 'economic activity rates').

Labour migrations and changing economic activity rates have always been important influences on the labour markets of the established industrial societies, and events since the Second World War, however dramatic, have in one sense repeated history. But when labour market history repeats itself the usual outcome is not continuity but flux and change.

According to Piore (1980), the highest estimates suggested that 'undocumented' migrant workers made up more than 10 per cent of the US labour force by the end of the 1970s. Most of these 'birds of passage' migrated from Latin America, especially Mexico and the Caribbean. A little earlier, Berger and Mohr (1975) had named the migrant worker (from North Africa, Turkey and other less developed countries) Western Europe's 'seventh man'. Indeed by 1970 the total of migrant workers in Western Europe was already near to 11 million, and some native European populations appeared to have given up doing manual work altogether since all of the menial work was now done by migrants. The small country of Switzerland accommodated nearly a million of them – 16 per cent of the total workforce (Castles and Kosack, 1973).

All economic activity rates fluctuate, but the most significant variation in activity rates in the established industrial societies has taken place amongst women. The UK census of 1851 revealed that 25 per cent of married women had paid work, but by the turn of the century the proportion had *dropped* to 10 per cent. During the First World War married women were drafted back into the labour force but when the war ended married women's activity rates fell back to pre-war levels (Beechey, 1986). Something similar happened during and after the Second World War, but in later years the proportion of married women in the labour force rose steadily so that by 1977 more than half of all married women in the United Kingdom were in paid work or were seeking employment.

The economic activity rates of British women can clearly go down as well as up, but it seems likely that the present level of female participation will be sustained and may even increase still further in the near future. The economic activity rates of women in the United States have changed in very much the same way as they have in the United Kingdom and similar trends can be observed in other established industrial societies. Some countries, for example Italy, have had a slower start, but even in Ireland – which has very low female economic activity rates by European standards – married women's activity rates increased from 7.5 per cent in 1971 to 17 per cent in 1981 (Jackson and Barry, 1989). Over roughly the same period West Germany experienced a significant increase in married women's activity rates and the activity rate for all women increased from 46.6 per cent to 51 per cent (Gensior and Schöler, 1989).

We now turn to the other 'side' of the labour market, to the demand for – rather than the supply of – labour. In large part, economic growth has ensured that there have been enough jobs for the new workers added to the labour forces of the established industrial societies, but the exceptions to this rule have always been painful and sometimes prolonged. The United Kingdom, for example, suffered mass unemployment throughout the 1980s. In the early years of the decade unemployment rates in the United States rose to nearly 10 per cent, while the Canadian rate exceeded 10 per cent (though still less than the UK rate of over 13 per cent; Ashton, 1986).

Such exceptions have often resulted from the disappearance of jobs, for example as a result of the oil price rises of the early 1970s and 1980, and the recession of the early 1980s. There are also additional problems of a chronic rather than acute nature. For example, as a result of economic competition and capital migration, there has been some redistribution of jobs between countries, including a redistribution of jobs to less developed countries which Fröbel *et al* (1980) called a 'new international division of labour'. This redistribution of jobs has brought unemployment to some of the established industrial countries. Similarly, some unemployment has been created where technological changes have reduced labour demand (for example, see Jordan, 1982).

Change in labour market conditions is not simply a question of changing numbers, the numbers of job-seekers and the number of vacancies. There have also been qualitative changes on both sides of the labour market. As far as the supply of labour is concerned, the most significant change has been an increase in the proportion of people who come to the labour market with pieces of paper which document their educational (academic or vocational) achievements – more and more workers have more and more of these *credentials*. Holding more credentials need not mean possessing more skills, however, and in cases such as the decline of apprenticeships in the United States and United Kingdom, some sections of the workforce appear to have become less skilled. There have also been less tangible changes in the sorts of people who use labour markets, for example changes in people's attitudes and expectations. The generations which first entered labour markets in the 1960s, 1970s and 1980s, for instance, did so with some different ideas of what they wanted from employment.

There have been two related and hugely important changes in the sorts of jobs which make up the demand side of the labour market. Both changes began, and have progressed further, in the United States, but have now affected all the established industrial countries: the shift of employment from manufacturing industry to the service sector and from blue-collar to white-collar jobs. But the outcomes of these two fundamental changes remain unclear since the evidence is often contradictory. For example, it is not at all clear how the shift to services and white-collar work has affected employers' requirements for workers with skills, or how the shift has affected the level of job security which employers feel able to offer. Furthermore, the impact of both trends is obscured by concurrent changes (for example in technology and work organisation) which also affect skill requirements and job security.

There is certainly less demand for undifferentiated (sometimes called 'unskilled') manual labour in factories in established industrial societies, but do the new white-collar jobs really require skilled workers? Interest in 'deskilling' increased after the publication of Braverman's (1974) account of the degradation of work in capitalist societies, and some writers (for example Crompton and Jones, 1984) have argued that white-collar work, just as much as manual labour in manufacturing, is deskilled work. Other commentators (for example Piore and Sabel, 1984) have reached the opposite conclusion: the new jobs which have been created in recent years have required 're-skilling' and 'multi-skilling' rather than workers with no skills at all.

The impact of the shift to service-sector and white-collar jobs on job security is also unclear, and once more the picture becomes more complicated when commentators find changes in management practices which might be independent of these shifts. In the 1980s some analysts (for example, Atkinson, 1984) thought that they might have identified a trend which heralded the disappearance of full-time, permanent jobs and of established career progression within a single company. On the other hand, others were beginning to ask whether such a trend would be welcomed. Dr Rosenmoller, of the West German Federal Labour Ministry, described this as the creation of a 'MacDonald's labour market', a damaging development which would certainly be resisted (Leadbeater and Lloyd, 1986, p. 126).

In part such faith in long-term employment and career structures, in the United States and the United Kingdom at least, stemmed from some commentators' (and employers') enthusiasm for Japanese employment practices – one of the factors they identified as the cause of Japanese economic success. Ironically, it soon appeared that the 'life-time' employment system of the Japanese (*nenkō*) had only ever been available to a minority of workers in that country, and was now out of favour with some employers (Kumazawa and Yamada, 1989).

There have also been big, but no less confusing, changes in the way labour markets are run. In different ways, countries like Japan, West Germany and Sweden have become committed to running labour markets in the interests of economic development. Typically, employers, financiers and labour unions have co-operated with the state in order to run labour markets in a way which will aid economic and social development, and development of the 'right' kind. This approach, sometimes described as 'corporatist', may have the welfare of the population somewhere in mind but is based on the conviction that labour markets work better if they are run by some body, usually the state, which will interfere in their operation and make plans for the future.

Other countries appear to be less convinced of the merits of interference and planning. Throughout the 1980s governments in the United States and the United Kingdom engaged in the deregulation of markets in general, but especially of labour markets. State interference in labour markets in these societies had never been quite of the type practised in West Germany or Japan. The interpreters of Beveridge and Roosevelt had more often seen state interference as justified by the failure of markets rather than as a way of making markets work. In the Reagan and Thatcher years, such interference was pronounced worse than useless and war was waged on those who wished to see labour markets regulated by the state or by anyone else (like the unions, for example).

At the time of writing, it seems that some of the Eastern European countries which rejected state socialism in the revolutions of 1989 will opt for the deregulated approach to labour markets when turning their economies into capitalist economies. Elsewhere politics and economics will affect labour markets in different ways. In South Africa, some aspects of state regulation of labour markets have disappeared as part of the state's effort to reform apartheid. In Europe, a new form of international regulation will follow the economic and political unification planned for the European Community in 1992 and beyond.

Governments, unions and firms appear to want to make labour markets their business in one way or another, but there are also other institutions who want to make a business out of labour markets, and their influence has generally increased in recent times. It is only in the last half of the twentieth century that most employers have come to accept that they might pay other firms to find labour for them. Employers in most of the established industrial countries are now able to use a variety of services which have usually been available to their counterparts in the United States for some time. With a telephone call they can now begin an executive 'head hunt' or hire a gang of manual workers, just as easily as they hire a temporary secretary for a week.

Finally, I have already above referred to a change in the way we think about labour markets, that is, to a change which might be seen to be independent of changes in labour market conditions, or in the way labour markets are run; a conceptual shift which might even have caused some of the substantive changes described above. Labour markets are also, it appears, grist to the ideologist's mill. Ideas about labour markets were, for example, central to the majority of the arguments of the 'new right' thinkers and 'market radicals' who helped to initiate and implement the deregulatory policies pursued by Reagan in the United States and Thatcher in the United Kingdom in the 1980s. So far, we have seen that deregulation meant stopping 'interference' by governments or anyone else, but interference in what? In the free play of 'market forces' of course.

This rationale is given flesh by 'supply-side economics' which identifies obstacles to improved economic performance on the supply side of the labour market, especially in a lack of competition between workers which limits the amount of labour (of the right type or at the right price) which is available to employers. According to the market radicals, all sorts of 'restrictive practices', but especially those operating in labour markets, are obstacles to improved economic performance. Such practices may have been intended to promote social justice or equality but cannot achieve such aims because they act as a brake on development.

Instead, the market mechanism must be freed from its fetters and we will then find that the mechanism itself will carry us towards an alternative goal to that of equality and justice – the goal of improved living standards for all. Such a goal is in fact the only realistic aim we can have, the only one that is achievable. The price for interfering in labour markets was paid in the form of lower growth and high wages and hence price inflation. In a misguided attempt to 'save' people from the market (for example, by making welfare benefits, or 'too generous' welfare benefits, available), governments had prevented the market from bringing benefits to the people.

In this way the market radicals are able to conclude their argument with the lesson they learnt from their master, Adam Smith, who taught that the 'invisible' hand of the market was rather more adept at distributing the resources required for growth and development than any human hand. At the time of writing, the 'Adam Smith' idea of a labour market is popular in the United States and in the United Kingdom and some Eastern European countries, but it is perhaps not the dominant view amongst the leaders of the most successful industrialised societies, namely Japan and West Germany, or amongst the most successful employers in the United States or United Kingdom (who have an eye on their German and Japanese competitors of course).

In Japan and West Germany, planners and policy-makers are not so much concerned with any *failure* of labour markets (although they may want the state to provide a safety net), but with giving a hand to the invisible hand: consciously improving labour markets to make capitalism work better. The apparent difference of opinion between established industrial societies, between those who spurn interference in labour markets and those who see a place for interference, might support the evidence for the growth of a new ideological division in the wake of the collapse of the older ideological battles between East and West.

It was once argued that this battle would be resolved in 'convergence': societies in the East and West were thought to be converging towards a new type of society in which planned economic development was pursued within a mixed economy (cf. Goldthorpe, 1984). Recent history suggests that convergence of this type may well occur between some societies in the East and some societies in the West, but also that convergence of another sort may also take place: between other societies in the East and West which are committed to an 'Adam Smith' vision of markets, and especially of labour markets.

There are, it seems, competing ideas about labour markets, and competition between these ideas can lead to one view or another becoming dominant at a particular time and in a particular place.

For much of the post-war period in the United Kingdom, for example, many people – although perhaps not so many of those with real influence (see MacInnes, 1987) – believed that free markets were anarchic and cruel. The one sure lesson that we can learn from the history of ideas about (labour) markets is that these ideas are not fixed and that yesterday's orthodoxies can quickly become tomorrow's heresies.[2]

WHAT IS A LABOUR MARKET?

The reader can be sure that if the foregoing has not excited their interest in labour markets, the subject is not to their taste and they should find another book to read. But any reader who has not been turned off will now want an answer to one, very important, question – how do we make sense of labour markets, how do we make sense of all the changes and the ideological differences described above? It is to the answer to this question that this book is supposed to contribute, but before the attempt is made something else is required. Up to this point labour markets have been discussed in an almost negligent way – as if every reader was clear about what was being discussed and every reader shared the same understanding of the subject. For reasons which will shortly be explained, a great deal more precision is now required in our thinking.

The authors of textbooks collect together the best thoughts and findings of other writers (and usually one or two of their own) and present them in a way which they hope will allow their readers to get the most out of the subject. This means that the textbook-writer has only two real problems to solve: which thoughts and findings should be included and how should they be organised? The question about organisation will be dealt with in Chapter 2, but the problem of selection is logically a priority. In order to select, one needs criteria, for example ideas of 'relevance', 'originality' and 'clarity' which help the textbook-writer to decide what (and who) to put in the book and what to leave out.

Surprisingly, the trickiest of these criteria turns out to be relevance. It is not always obvious how one decides which thoughts and findings are relevant to the subject. This is a particular problem when, as with a book on the sociology of labour markets, there are no established textbooks already on the shelves.[3] In this case, there is unlikely to be much agreement about how the subject should be defined, but without a definition how can one decide what is relevant to it? So, we will have to begin with a definition of the subject matter, and do this knowing that some people will disagree with the definition; and in the fear that the definition may be so wide that it overlaps with established fields of study, or so narrow that it makes the subject seem trivial.

An abstract definition of the labour market – the hiring fair

In *Far From The Madding Crowd*,[4] Thomas Hardy describes a 'hiring fair' in his fictional English town of Casterbridge. Such fairs were held throughout the countryside into the nineteenth century, and it was at hiring fairs that farmers hired agricultural workers for a season or for a longer period:

At the end of the street stood from two to three hundred blithe and hearty labourers waiting upon Chance – all men of the stamp to whom labour suggests nothing worse than a wrestle with gravitation, and pleasure nothing better than a renunciation of the same. Among these, carters and waggoners were distinguished by having a piece of whip-cord twisted round their hats; thatchers wore a fragment of woven straw; shepherds held their sheep-crooks in their hands; and thus the situation required was known to the hirers at a glance.

The hiring fair is an example of a labour market and it is as good an example as any to use to work up a definition of the labour market in the abstract.

The abstract labour market is actually made up of five logically distinct processes, but each of these processes also involves a relationship. Each process is two-sided, like a coin, since there are always two possibilities in the labour market: something done by the person who wants work and something done by the prospective employer. The meaning of this riddle will become clear as we consider each of the five processes in turn, but first readers must make a mental note of an important point that they should bear in mind throughout this book.

In common with the rest of the literature on the sociology of labour markets, this book is biased. It is biased towards the happier labour market event of hiring and away from the more dismal event of firing. Nevertheless, everything that is said in general terms about labour market processes (both here and in the chapters that follow) applies equally well in principle to both recruitment and 'separations' (Norris, 1978b) from employment including redundancies (voluntary and compulsory), dismissals and voluntary quits. Thus the five labour market processes described below are as useful, as abstractions, for understanding how people leave employment as they are for understanding how people enter employment. Readers should simply think of each process operating in reverse, and culminating not in an offer to buy or sell labour but in a separation from employment.

We begin with the process of *informing employers*. Employers must learn that workers are available for employment. At the hiring fair, workers conveyed this information simply by standing in the street. The shepherds and thatchers who had tramped many miles to the market town, 'told' their prospective employers that they wanted to work ('required a situation') simply by attending the fair. But, since any labour market process is always a relationship, the process of informing employers need not be undertaken by the workers seeking jobs. For example, employers can be informed by making their own direct approach to workers: by stopping passers-by, by 'cold-calling' on the telephone and so on.

In the second labour market process, workers must learn that jobs are available, in other words there is a process of *informing workers*. At the hiring fair workers were informed in the same way as employers: by the presence of the farmers (who did not tramp but came on horseback) at the fair, they knew jobs were available. Once more, there is another side to the coin: workers can be informed through their own efforts rather than those of employers, by cold-calling on their own behalf, for example.

The third and fourth processes are commonly called *screening*. In the process of *screening workers*, the employer gets hold of sufficient information to allow him or her to decide whether or not a particular worker should be offered a particular job. Employers can screen workers by asking questions. At the Casterbridge hiring fair they asked workers how far they had come to be at the fair, and what their previous employment had been. But at the hiring fair the workers also contributed to the process. They might be 'all men of the [same] stamp' but by the whipcord round their hats, and the woven straw and shepherd's crooks they sported, the 'blithe and hearty labourers' screened themselves: this man was suitable for the sheepfold but not for the stable, another would do for a thatcher but was of no interest to an employer with no roofs to thatch.

Once approached by a prospective employer at the hiring fair, the job-seeker might respectfully ask what his duties would be should he take the situation, how much pay, and what food and lodging he should expect? Such questions are part of a process of *screening employers*, in which workers gather more information (than the simple knowledge of a vacancy) in order to decide whether they should accept a particular vacancy. Once more the other party can contribute to the process. When employers place advertisements which describe the kind of company they run, their pay scales, career structures and so on, they are screening themselves by providing additional information to job-seekers.

The final labour market process is the specific *offer* to buy or sell labour. As before, there are two possibilities: the offer may be an offer to buy ('an offer of employment') or an offer to sell. The *offer of employment* is, of course, made by the employer: at the hiring fair, the farmer will ask the worker whether he will accept the vacant situation. The *offer to sell labour* is made by the job-seeker: the shepherd says he would be happy to tend the master's flocks if it pleases the farmer.

It might be argued that the conclusion of the transaction – the actual buying and selling of labour – does not take place until work begins. It is only then that workers really find out what labour is actually required of them, and what they will get in return. Similarly, the employer will only find out when work begins how much labour and what type of labour has actually been bought. It could therefore be argued that what goes on in work should also fall within the subject matter of the sociology of the labour market since this is where labour is really exchanged.

I have taken the view that such a broad definition would trespass on other fields of study, notably the sociology of work. It seems to me that the study of the working-out of contractual arrangements is the first act of the sociology of work, rather than the last act of the sociology of labour markets. This distinction has one important consequence which readers might note. According to the definition used here, several related areas which are of great interest to sociology are not directly relevant to the sociology of labour markets. Most obviously, the negotiation of wages and conditions for, or by, people in work is only relevant so far as negotiations affect the five labour market processes, or the labour market processes affect these negotiations.

The limits of an abstract definition of the labour market

It must be obvious to any reader who has ever been in the labour market that there are serious faults in an abstract definition which is made up of a description of five logically distinct processes (also see Harris, 1984). In the first place, it is quite possible for one or more processes to occur simultaneously. Indeed this is exactly what happened at Hardy's hiring fair: some simultaneous screening – of workers and employers – was accomplished through the wearing of favours. To take another example, a press advertisement which details what the employer expects of the successful applicant for a vacancy screens as well as informs job-seekers. In fact some labour market processes can be so perfunctory that they appear to be implicit or to have hardly happened at all. For instance, is it really screening when an employer of unskilled labour fills vacancies on a 'first come first served' basis?

In the second place, even if labour market processes do occur separately and consecutively, there is no guarantee that they will occur in the order described above. For example, Gabriel Oak, one of Hardy's characters in *Far From the Madding Crowd*, comes to the hiring fair to offer himself in the 'superior position' of a bailiff. By doing this, he is screening employers – warning off those who only want shepherds and so on – *before* learning of what offers of employment are to be had. This is not an unusual order of events but it costs Gabriel Oak dear – he spends nearly the whole day at the fair without success. Belatedly he reverses the order and sets himself up as a shepherd (spending what little money he has on a crook and exchanging his overcoat for a shepherd's smockcoat) when he realises that most of the prospective employers seem to want a man to tend their sheep. Nor does this alternative plan bring success, however:

Gabriel wished he had not nailed up his colours as a shepherd, but had laid himself out for anything in the whole cycle of labour that was required in the fair.

Thirdly, the processes may be gone through in two different orders by employers and workers. For example, on the strength of the hoped-for success of this book, I call a professor in Boston, Massachusetts, and say I want a job. I have already reached the offer to sell labour, but the worthy professor may not even have considered whether he or she has a vacancy. Fourthly, at the hiring fair every process was gone through in a day (sometimes more than once). This is not necessary at all, though it might help us to avoid the nervous upset of waiting between application and interview, and interview and decision, if it *were* always necessary.

Finally, if they need not occur over a specified period of time, still less do labour market processes have to occur in the same place. The hiring fair was held in a literal *market place*, but some labour markets do not have a single physical location. News-papers, telephones, and letters help us to make this unnecessary. It is possible for the labour market to have a physical location – the hiring halls of 'referral' labour unions in the United States for example – but it is more often the case in established industrial societies that they do not.

For example, where is the labour market for advertising personnel? We do not see unemployed advertising people standing around on Madison Avenue or in Covent Garden (with a row of felt tip pens in a well-tailored breast pocket to distinguish their calling), not with any serious hope of being hired anyway. You might say the physical location of the labour market for these people is in a number of offices, wine bars, or sports clubs, but what about the vacancy pages of *Adweek*? You might hear of the job in the press, offer yourself for it in a letter, be offered it in an office, and think it over and accept it in a telephone call from home.

Labour markets need have neither a fixed time nor a fixed place, but they must have some sort of time and place otherwise how could people use them? If they do not know when and where, workers cannot find jobs and employers cannot hire workers. The ways in which times and places are established, and in which workers and employers come to hear of them, will be investigated in later chapters. But even if workers and employers learn of the time and place of a labour market, they may not be able to use it because it is also necessary for them to find the *right* labour market.

WHICH LABOUR MARKET?

The problem of finding the right labour market, and its solution, can be illustrated by considering the methods government agencies use to quantify labour markets in a way which makes sense to the people, both workers and employers, who use them.

Everyone agrees that quantifying labour markets involves counting labour supply and demand, but there is no simple or obvious answer to the question of what should be included in these counts. When governments first began to produce social and economic statistics, for example, they wanted some sort of country-wide counting system. This was why, after all, the term *state*-istics was coined. Now agencies can count the numbers of unemployed, and the numbers of vacancies, on a country-wide basis, and so can quantify, for example, the 'United States labour market'. But is the 'United States labour market' real, is it the sort of labour market that people can use?

Who, in the United States, thinks on a national scale when they want to find a job, fill a vacancy or even plan policy or open a private employment agency? The 'United States labour market' is a statistical fiction as far as most people are concerned, but what about the few for whom it is a real possibility to consider vacancies from coast to coast? For most of *them* it would be just as easy to move abroad for a job, perhaps easier than moving from Rhode Island to the Midwest. So why not quantify a 'World labour market'? This is fine as long as we realise that such a concept makes little sense to a redundant steelworker in Pittsburgh, South Wales or Lorraine.[5]

When government agencies attempt to quantify labour markets in a way which makes sense to most of the people who use them, they usually come up with some notion of the 'local labour market'. For example, it is assumed that most people do not want to move house, and therefore that when they are looking for a job they will do so within a reasonable daily travelling distance. The 'travel-to-work-area' around a settlement is then defined as that settlement's 'local labour market'. This is an imperfect solution in both theory and practice. It is a crude device for something so complex but with luck it might make sense to most of the people most of the time, and the important point to note is that this operational definition gives a labour market a (more or less inaccurate, more or less arbitrary) sphere or territory, and (therefore) a boundary.

We establish the territories of labour markets by asking which labour market are we talking about, which labour market do we want to quantify? Thus, if government agencies answer that they want to talk about the local labour market, then they will use an idea like 'travel-to-work-area' in order to quantify it. They will give the labour market a territory (and a boundary). But there is more than one way to answer the question 'which labour market?'.

One of the most frequent problems encountered in trying to quantify a local labour market (by defining a travel-to-work-area for example) is that what people see as the geographical location of the labour market tends to vary. We have already seen that not all the residents of Pittsburgh think their labour market is limited by the neighbourhood or even the metropolitan area. Furthermore, this variation is often systematic, that is, it varies with another factor, like *occupation*. For example, senior executives may be more likely than ex-steelworkers to think of a country-wide or even world-wide labour market. Why does the definition and boundary of the labour market vary with occupation? Because occupations are also sorts of 'territories' for labour markets with their own boundaries.

It is for this reason that government agencies list labour market statistics (counts of supply and demand) by occupation as well as by location, but occupation and location are not the only variables which agencies use to tabulate their statistics. For example, many agencies break their labour supply figures down according to the gender, 'race' or ethnic origin of job-seekers. For whatever reason – including discrimination by employers (see Chapter 3 below) –

gender, 'race' and ethnic origin also provide answers to the question 'which labour market?'; they are also labour market territories or spheres with their own boundaries. Two examples should illustrate this point: the first compares gender territories to geographical territories, the second compares gender territories to occupational territories.

Firstly, when they are using travel-to-work-areas to quantify 'local labour markets', statisticians may well find that they need to define *two* travel-to-work-areas, one for men and one for women, for each locality. If they are quantifying the labour market of a settlement which is dominated by heavy industry, for instance, they may find that the travel-to-work-area for women who live in that settlement must actually be extended to include a neighbouring town where most of the women find their (service sector) jobs (cf. Fevre, 1989b).

Secondly, occupational breakdowns by government agencies commonly group together women's jobs in a smaller number of occupational categories than men's jobs (see Equal Opportunities Commission, 1986, for example). They do this for two reasons. In the first place, women workers are not distributed across the whole range of occupations in the same way as men are. In the second, official statistics exaggerate the 'clustering' of women's jobs because the societies in which these agencies operate generally attach less status to – for instance, see less 'skill' in – women's jobs, and so are less likely to distinguish between these jobs. For *both* of these reasons, occupational breakdowns of labour market statistics make much more sense when they are also tabulated by gender (and also by 'race', ethnic origin and so on).

The various ways in which government agencies tabulate their figures illustrate many of the possible answers to the question 'which labour market?'. Each variable helps us to specify what people (both workers and employers) see as *their* labour market, the labour market that makes most sense, is most useful, to them. Yet official statistics cannot cope with every possible sort of territory (and boundary) of labour markets.

For example, 'company people' (with all sorts of different occupations, ages and so on) in the United States or Japan, or in the UK Civil Service, see their labour markets as being located within a single employer. Thus the demand for labour which is relevant to them consists in the vacancies which appear in internal bulletins. Such people see the territory of their labour market as identical with their firm, but no government agency would contemplate tabulating published vacancy statistics separately for each firm and organisation. Similarly, no government agency would tabulate labour supply statistics according to the names of the labour unions which people join, yet union membership can also constitute a territory of, and set a boundary for, a labour market (see Chapter 4 below).

Some government agencies do try to reflect this complexity in their figures. They tabulate vacancies according to whether they are filled on the open market or not, and according to whether they are notified to a public employment service or not. Agencies also tabulate vacancies according to the different qualifications or training that employers say they require of new recruits. Similarly, when counting labour supply, agencies can try to count those people who want new jobs but are currently employed, as well as those who are unemployed (a complex concept in itself). When they count the unemployed, they can count workers according to their qualifications and training, and according to the way in which they became unemployed: those made redundant, those who were dismissed, those finishing temporary contracts, and those entering the labour market for the first time or re-entering after a break.

If they do all of these things agencies will help to provide answers to the question 'which labour market?', but even the most sophisticated statistics will inadequately reflect the complexity of real labour markets, the diversity of labour market territories. In later chapters of this book, the investigation of this empirical diversity will be just as important as any further discussion of the abstract nature of the labour market described above. Because they have a profound effect on people's lives, we must also try to understand the systematic basis of real labour market territories like locality, occupation, gender, 'race' and age.

WHY ARE LABOUR MARKETS RELEVANT TO SOCIOLOGY?

This chapter began with a description of extensive social and economic changes which would excite the interest of any but the most apathetic social scientist, but why should sociologists, in particular, find the study of labour markets useful? Chapter 2 will ask why sociology is relevant to labour markets and show that different social sciences can find labour markets relevant for different reasons. Economists, for example, are interested in labour markets because they – like other markets – provide a mechanism for the distribution of resources. Economists' main concerns often centre on the way in which the price of labour is set, that is, they are interested in the effect of labour markets on wages. In general, sociologists have not been interested in labour markets for these reasons.

Sociologists are not so much concerned with wage-setting as with how different people end up in particular jobs (or with no jobs at all). Wages are obviously of some interest to sociologists – the level of pay is often what distinguishes one job from another, for example – but they are not the central concern. Whereas economists seek to develop better theories of how labour markets set wages, sociologists are more interested in how labour markets put some people in 'good' jobs, others in 'bad' jobs, and some people on welfare benefits.

These issues concern sociologists who study labour markets because they are actually of considerable importance to the whole discipline of sociology (see also Offe, 1985). In most areas of sociological enquiry theorists and researchers have found that whether or not people use labour markets, and what happens as a result of their labour market activity, are of great importance. There are few sociological fields in which it is completely irrelevant whether or not the people being studied are dependent on paid employment or have private means; are in work or are unemployed; or are in one occupation and not another. For example, even the most unsophisticated, undergraduate survey of any set of social attitudes will usually divide the population sample into unemployed and employed, and probably also into blue-collar and white-collar workers.

Finally, while the results of labour market processes have always been of interest to sociologists working in any number of different areas, in recent years this interest has become more intense – and more concerned with theorising the operation of the labour market – as the discipline has rediscovered the relevance of *all* things economic. Durkheim, Marx and Weber believed that an understanding of such things was of fundamental importance and their books are full of 'economic sociology'. But for much of the twentieth century, and especially in the United States and United Kingdom, many of the successors of Durkheim, Marx and Weber seemed to believe that the 'founding fathers' of sociology had said all there was to say about these economic fundamentals.

To show that this was no longer the case by the 1980s, one need only point to the proliferation of new journals and research projects which were broadly concerned with economic sociology. In the United Kingdom, for instance, a major new journal, *Work, Employment and Society*, was launched by the British Sociological Association in 1987, while the *Social Change and Economic Life Research Initiative* – involving researchers from fourteen UK universities – had begun in the preceding year.

SUMMARY

What happens in the labour market is of vital importance to most of the world's people, including those of us who live in established industrial societies. These societies have recently witnessed some dramatic changes: in labour market conditions, in the way labour markets are run, and in the way labour markets are thought of or theorised. All of these changes have sparked disputes about the facts and controversy about the evaluation of these facts (usually taking the form of an argument about whether the changes have been good or bad).

In order to make sense of labour markets, and of labour market changes, it was first necessary to define the subject of study as five labour market processes beginning with *informing employers* and ending with *the offer to sell labour* (not forgetting separations from employment). But this abstract definition has limitations: in the real world it is not necessary for the labour market processes to occur consecutively, in any particular order, or at a particular time or in a particular place.

In the discussion of attempts to describe real labour markets in a useful way – and of operational definitions of labour markets – which followed, the idea of labour market territories was introduced. Some of the territories were real, geographical locations, but others relied on differences in occupation, gender and so on. Such territories are at least of equal interest to us as the (abstract) labour processes themselves.

Finally, this chapter explained why all of the foregoing was relevant to sociology. The huge and complex, social and economic changes described above provide one answer, but it can also be shown that labour markets are vital to general sociological concerns, and that there has been a recent shift within the discipline towards renewed interest in 'economic sociology', of which the sociology of labour markets is a key component.

The following chapters will describe the contribution of this 'key component' by attempting to show exactly how sociology can help us to make sense of the workings of labour markets, and of change in labour markets, in established industrial societies. While abstract definitions and empirical descriptions may be interesting in themselves, they are really only the first, preliminary steps on a long and fascinating journey. We begin this journey with a short-cut, however – a short-cut that takes us (very briefly) into a strange land, the land of economics.

NOTES

1. Although readers should note that a hard-and-fast distinction between events in underdeveloped countries and events in established industrial countries is misleading. For example, some readers may conclude that events in underdeveloped countries can be interpreted as signs of the first, faltering steps these societies are taking towards capitalist development; whereas events in established industrial countries are to be seen as (in part) the results of change in the nature of 'mature' capitalist societies. This conclusion is flawed in two respects. Firstly, changes in the nature of established industrial societies have had considerable effects on underdeveloped countries. Secondly, events in underdeveloped countries can often alter events in established industrial countries.
2. If ideas can change the world, so can the world change ideas. I am indebted to one of my anonymous referees who points out the lesson of this observation for the 'market radicals' who do not seem to be aware that fashions in ideas may be affected by economic changes, for example by changes in labour market conditions.

3. At the time of writing there is no proper undergraduate textbook on the sociology of labour markets, but there has, of course, been much general writing on the subject. Of those volumes published in English, Ashton, 1986 and Berg, 1981 are perhaps the best known.
4. Penguin edition, Harmondsworth, 1979, pp. 88–90.
5. Although it might make rather more sense to the son or daughter of a Kashmiri farmer who has worked in Norway, the United Kingdom and Kuwait.

2

ECONOMICS, SOCIOLOGY AND THE
STUDY OF LABOUR MARKETS

If we now have some idea why labour markets are relevant to
sociology, we do not yet know why sociology is relevant to the
study of labour markets. Our short-cut consists in a discussion of
labour market economics – by far the most productive (to date) of
the social sciences which have shown an interest in labour
markets. We will look briefly (and with inexpert eyes) at the basic
principles of this branch of economics, and will survey the opinion
of some leading schools of economic thought which offer
different, but equally powerful, analyses of labour markets from
the economists' viewpoint. We will then be able to progress to a
description of the sociological approach, conceived not as an
alternative to the economists' approach but as a contribution to
the interdisciplinary study of labour markets. The chapter
concludes with the promised answer to the question of organisation (see p. 9 above), in the shape of an overview of the remainder
of the book.

LABOUR MARKET ECONOMICS

It will do no harm to remind the reader that this section is very
basic, is not written by an expert, and that the literature on labour
market economics is vast. Economists may find little in this section
that is to their liking: here a sociologist writes of economics in as
nearly a perfunctory way as Becker, the economist, writes of
sociology and all other social science that is not neo-classical

economics (see Becker, 1976; and Hodgson, 1988, pp. 117–8). Readers who require more expert discussion must read the work of the economists for themselves.[1]

The first thing to make clear is that labour market economics does not have quite the same subject matter as labour market sociology. The key to the economists' approach lies in the term 'labour *market*'. Any buying and selling activity can be called a 'market' and the term 'labour market' simply indicates what is being sold – labour rather than the products of labour (goods and services), or currencies for example. In any market there is an *exchange* between at least two people, one who buys and one who sells. There need be no more than one seller and one buyer (so the market need not involve competition between buyers or between sellers), and it need not involve the exchange of labour for money. For example, labour may be exchanged for bed and board, or a promise to write off debts. There must, however, be some exchange, and pure physical compulsion to labour, for instance, is not enough to make a market.

In Chapter 1 the conclusion of the labour market transaction, the actual buying and selling of labour, was specifically excluded from the subject matter of the sociology of labour markets. This was done because a wider definition would have trespassed into other established areas of sociology, especially the sociology of work, but labour market economists were never so faint-hearted. Although they are interested in the five labour market processes described in Chapter 1, these economists are usually only interested in the five processes so far as they contribute to the exchange of labour.

Economists are interested in labour markets for the same reason that they are interested in all markets: because they provide, through exchange, a mechanism for the distribution of resources. Exchange involves the setting of a price. Although this need not be a price in money, economists have frequently concentrated their attention on the money-price set for exchange. In the case of labour markets, then, they have concentrated on the way in which wages are set, and their theories are largely about the effect of labour markets on wage rates.

Economists were initially concerned to develop a theory that would explain both wage setting and the levels of labour supply and demand in a particular type of labour market. The type they had in mind was rather like the 'hiring fair' described in Chapter 1, a market with numerous buyers and sellers. At the most basic level, economic theory tells us that in such labour markets – as in any other market with numerous buyers and sellers – the price of the thing being sold will be determined (or, at least, heavily influenced) by the 'laws of supply and demand'.

Most economists would recognise the message, while perhaps deploring the bald manner in which that message is stated, of this succinct exposition of economic theory:

The market for labour is not much different from the market for bananas; if demand exceeds supply, the price of the product should increase; if supply exceeded demand, the reverse should happen and the price should fall; at some point demand should equal supply at an equilibrium point.

(Stoney quoted by Canning, 1984)

All other things being equal – as economists are fond of saying – the price of labour (for example the level of wages) will be low if there are more sellers than buyers, in other words, if the supply of labour exceeds the demand for it. Conversely, the price of labour will be higher if demand exceeds supply. The most important 'other thing' that has to be 'equal' is competition. The 'laws of supply and demand' work in this way because there is competition within each group: competition over labour between the buyers, and competition over jobs between the sellers of labour. So far so good, but what was the meaning of 'an equilibrium point' in the quotation?

We must remember that this economic theory is a theory of the way in which levels of supply and demand are determined, as well as a theory of price-setting. All other things being equal, supply and demand adjust to each other *through* the price mechanism. For example, if there are more sellers than buyers the price will fall so that less people find it an attractive idea to sell their labour and/or more people want to buy labour. A similar adjustment occurs where demand exceeds supply: more people want to sell labour and/or less people want to buy it because the price of labour is rising. Sooner or later these adjustments will make supply and demand equal each other – the market will find just the right price at which the same number of people want to sell as want to buy. This is the market's 'equilibrium point'.

It seems that, in practice, markets are rarely 'in equilibrium' and more often in the process of adjustment; but this observation need not invalidate economic theory because markets are said to be always adjusting towards the equilibrium point. Even if they never find this point, the way in which markets set wages and levels of supply and demand can be explained in terms of this movement towards equilibrium.

Economists are agreed thus far, but no further, that the market for labour is like the market for bananas. Many economists think that in the real world, as opposed to the economics textbook, 'all other things' are very rarely equal, and if economists are to understand labour markets they must pay attention to the 'other things' rather than to the laws of supply and demand which may look good in theory but are so obscured in practice as to explain very little. The most important 'other thing' that most of these economists would point to as the best hope for explanation is the limitation, or even absence, of competition in real labour markets with numerous buyers and sellers.

If competition does not exist, the laws of supply and demand will not work. For example, the price of labour need not be low, even if there are more sellers than buyers, if the sellers have agreed not to compete with each other (none of them is going to undercut the price in order to get a job). If this happens the market cannot adjust towards equilibrium; the price mechanism which is supposed to do the trick cannot work – the price cannot move – and so the market is stuck in 'disequilibrium' with supply exceeding demand. This particular example presents a more realistic picture of what happens in some labour markets than the basic theory according to some economists, discussed later in this chapter. They say that real markets are either stuck in disequilibrium or, far from moving towards equilibrium, are actually moving away from it. As a result, there is unemployment and, since employers are short of labour and/or are paying too much for it, low production.

There are many ways in which economists attempt to bridge the gap between wage-setting in real labour markets and their basic, simple theory. Their various solutions to the problem will be mentioned in several of the following chapters, but here we will only consider two types of solution. Both types were fore-shadowed in Chapter 1 when we discussed the question of 'which labour market?' in order to help bridge the gap between an abstract definition and empirical description of labour markets. There we saw that, in practice, one person's labour market was not always another person's labour market. Some economists have argued that the solution to this 'problem' lies in the role of the *institutions* which affect the operation of labour markets. Others have argued that the investigation of the behaviour of *individuals* will provide a solution to the problem. We begin with this latter type of theory.

Human capital

Business-people who want to increase output and/or profits often choose to increase investment. This means that they put more money (their own or someone else's) into the operation, thereby increasing their 'capital'. This can be done in several ways, for example you can invest in more or better machines or in buildings. Sometimes the investment does not pay off, but the logic behind it is clear: if you have more capital you have a better chance of increasing output and/or profits.

Economists are, of course, very interested in business practices, and it is perfectly understandable that they should apply the logic that seems to inform business decisions to the decisions made by ordinary people. Thus Becker (1962, 1975) claimed that ordinary people also made decisions about 'investment' in the expectation of greater 'output' and 'profits'. But people did not, obviously, invest in machines or buildings; instead they invested in themselves – they tried to increase their '*human* capital' by undergoing education and training.

There is a limit, of course, to how much human capital people will choose to invest in because, as with any other investment, they must consider the potential costs as well as benefits. You *may* gain in the long run by investing in education, but you will definitely lose in the short run. You will lose because you will forgo opportunities to earn income while you are acquiring extra human capital.[2] You may even have to borrow money – and pay interest on it – in order to invest in education or training. Basically, if you invest in human capital you will be poor (and perhaps miserable) for a while before (if you are lucky) your investment pays off.

It is assumed that the benefits of such investment are realised in the form of higher income later on because more human capital makes people more productive – they can produce more, or do more demanding jobs. If I leave school unable to read or write, I will not have added to my human capital in the same way as a qualified physician or someone with an MBA, but exactly how does their investment pay off? We assume that it pays off for employers because more human capital means more productive workers and, just like more productive machines, more productive workers will increase output and profits. We can now see how the employer can pay more – they have the means to reward someone's investment in their own human capital – but why should they pay more? The answer lies in the labour market.

In the basic, 'laws of supply and demand', theory described above it was assumed that labour supply and demand were *homogeneous*: all workers were the same and all jobs were interchangeable. But in the real world (as we saw in Chapter 1) this is patently untrue. There are different categories of supply and demand, including different categories of supply and demand for different levels of education and training. In the terms of human capital theory, we assume that labour supply differs according to the degree to which job-seekers have invested in their human capital, and that jobs differ in terms of the human-capital investment required of the workers who do them.

Since not everyone has the same human capital, those with more of it are 'in greater demand'. This does not mean that there are more jobs for them, or even that demand exceeds supply in these jobs, but that their labour market will be 'tighter'. That is, whatever the state of supply and demand in general, the labour market for people with higher human capital will look more promising from the job-seeker's point of view. For example, if labour supply exceeds demand everywhere, the gap will be less for workers with higher human capital.

According to the laws of supply and demand, we might expect that this should not be the case – labour market conditions should not vary in this way. But because of the investment (in human capital) decisions taken by workers, job-seekers cannot move around the labour market as the laws of supply and demand predict. For example, job-seekers cannot stop looking for vacancies in jobs where supply exceeds demand, and start applying for jobs where higher human capital is needed and the gap between supply and demand is small or non-existent. They cannot do this because their labour is not equivalent and so it will not satisfy the employers' demand. As a result, wages cannot adjust downwards as the laws of supply and demand would lead us to believe: higher human capital will therefore get the higher wages we have already assumed that employers can afford.

Differences in human capital limit the possibilities of competition between employers just as they limit competition between job-seekers. For instance, employers who require workers with high human capital will not compete for other workers and so the demand for the labour of these other workers is low. Just as labour supply cannot move freely around the labour market, following the laws of supply and demand, labour demand is similarly constrained. There is no flood of demand to mop up excess labour supply of workers with low human capital and so their wages stay low.

The result of all this smart thinking is a theory which does not violate the basic laws of supply and demand – they would operate if they could – and therefore makes economic sense. Yet the theory is believed to make economic theory as a whole more adequate, in other words the theoretical abstractions more accurately reflect the real world. In real labour markets workers and jobs are not all the same and, in this theory, these differences are theorised with the concept of 'human capital'.

Yet some problems remain; most obviously, why – according to the theory – should differences in human capital persist? For example, why don't workers who have little human capital get more of it and so make the differences between categories of labour supply disappear? If labour supply became homogeneous there would be no limits on competition, the laws of supply and demand would be unhindered, and the market would adjust towards equilibrium.

To deal with this problem, which is not after all merely an abstract one because differences in education and training do persist in the real world, economists have made a variety of additional assumptions. Some (see, for example, Joll *et al.*, 1983) assume that differences in human capital reflect differences in abilities. Other economists point out that there are systematic variations in the amount of human capital which people appear to have: there seem to be hidden patterns behind people's choices about human capital.

For instance, those who choose to do MBAs may have other things in common apart from this decision, and things which distinguish them from those who cannot read or write. Sowell (1981a, 1981b), for example, argues that people who are members of minority groups will be less likely to invest in education and training if they think they are going to suffer discrimination in recruitment or promotion. Thus, the employment patterns of minority Americans can be explained – in part[3] – by their historical underinvestment in human capital (Sowell, 1981b, p. 262).

The idea of human capital allows further elaboration of economic theory to make it a better fit with reality while not violating the laws of supply and demand. For example, the importance of occupations in real labour markets can be theorised as the result of the different human capital requirements of different jobs. Furthermore, explanations of systematic variations in the acquisition of human capital can help economic theory to explain the employment patterns of blacks and women, for example.

Human capital theory makes economic theory a more adequate explanation of real labour markets, but it is fair to say that not all of the developments associated with this theory have been universally welcomed by economists, and have sometimes provoked hostile reaction from sociologists. Sociologists have often seen human capital theory as not so much an explanation as an attempt to legitimate inequality. Inequality in income, for example, sometimes seems – in the terms of the theory – to be the outcome of voluntary choices, including the choices made by people who appear to opt for lower incomes. Some sociologists, especially sociologists working in Europe, consider that this sounds rather too much like 'blaming the victims' for their own misfortunes. These sociologists have usually been more enthusiastic about *some* statements of the second type of theory which attempts to bridge the gap between basic economic theory and the empirical evidence – the type which attends to the role of institutions rather than to the behaviour of individuals.

Institutional Theories

For four decades (see for example, Reynolds, 1951) there have been suggestions that basic economic theory is mistaken when it assumes that it is safe to talk about *one* labour market, even at the most abstract level. A variety of terms have been coined to convey this disquiet, and readers can be forgiven for being a little confused about the precise differences between 'balkanised', 'dual', 'split', 'segmented' and 'structured' labour markets. At the most basic level, however, theses terms are interchangeable. They are all meant to imply that basic economic theory – the laws of supply and demand – fails to take into account the important observation of Chapter 1 that one person's labour market is not always another person's labour market.

Now this was also the concern of the economists who developed human capital theory, but whereas they pointed to the differences between individual workers and between individual jobs, economists who criticise the notion of a single labour market for all job-seekers and all employers point to the role of institutions which they think lies behind many of the differences between individuals and between jobs. To make this distinction as clear as possible, let us say that the argument in the preceding section suggested that differences between workers or jobs led to limitations on competition, whereas the argument here is that the role of institutions means that there is no one, unified labour. market.

If the distinction between this section and the preceding one is now clear, a word or two should be said about distinctions *within* this section. The two theories discussed here – 'radical' and 'Austrian' – are sometimes seen as alternatives, even as naturally antagonistic to each other. For whatever reason this assumption of antagonism is made, the most obvious difference between the two schools of thought lies in a simple matter of emphasis. 'Radical' theories give more emphasis to the role of institutions on the demand side of the labour market, while the 'Austrian' school emphasises the role of institutions on the supply side. We begin with the 'radical' economists.

The contribution of the self-styled 'radical' economists – who began to publish their ideas, in the United States, in the early

1970s – is best understood by way of a discussion of two key ideas advanced by the school: 'internal labour markets' and 'dual labour markets'. Both ideas are intended, as before, to add the necessary sophistication which will allow economics to bridge the gap between basic theory and empirical evidence, especially evidence of the labour market territories described in Chapter 1. Both ideas attempt to bridge the gap in the same way: by arguing that institutions on the demand side of the labour market lead to the creation of labour markets that are not unified.

In the first radical economics book, Doeringer and Piore (1971) observed that not all job vacancies were filled on the open market. Some employers filled their vacancies internally, and, more importantly, some employers had an established procedure for doing so. This procedure looked enough like a system to deserve a name of its own and so the term 'internal labour market' was applied.

The characteristics of internal labour markets (ILMs) vary, but the typical system is usually thought to have one 'point of entry', a training programme and an established career ladder (even though that ladder may be very short). In any event, the consequence of such a system is that existing employees are recruited to the better jobs in the firm or organisation.

Explanations for the existence of ILMs vary too. It is sometimes suggested that a mix of ILM and open-market recruitment represents a management strategy of 'divide and rule'. Where ILMs are combined with higher pay (see below), it is also suggested that these systems allow employers' to buy off their most dangerous adversaries, for example the most strongly unionised workers. But the most common explanation does not rely on assumptions about strategy or exigency. Instead, ILMs are said to reflect the fact that labour supply is not homogeneous.

This sounds like a familiar point, but the radical economists do not argue that labour supply differs according to the 'human capital' that workers decide to invest in themselves. Instead, they are concerned with the skills which employers decide to give workers. In the extreme example, the employer gives workers transferable skills, that is, skills which would be useful in another job with another firm. At some cost to their employer, therefore, workers have been given skills that make them more attractive to other employers. ILMs provide one way in which these workers can be tied to their current employer and thus they ensure that the benefits of training investment pay off, while making sure that others (competitors after all) do not reap the benefits of something they did not sow.

ILMs allow employers to produce skilled workers out of the job-seekers they recruit (on the open market) and, hopefully, allow employers to retain the workers they have trained. They will stay because of their prospects of promotion but also because they are well paid. Clearly, employers may consciously decide to pay higher wages to retain workers, but if they use an ILM they may not actually have the choice. Such employers will not wait until demand exceeds the supply of labour on the open market before paying higher wages because the labour market conditions that matter are those which prevail *within* the ILM. Since job-seekers in the open market cannot apply for internal vacancies (but only for admission at the 'point of entry'), ILMs insulate the workers who occupy them from competition and the price of their labour is higher as a result.

Obviously, not all employers use ILMs, so what of the employers who do not use them? If ILMs are so valuable why are they not universal? More importantly – at least so far as economic theory is concerned – do the laws of supply and demand work in the way the basic economic theory would predict where there are no ILMs? The radical economists say that when ILMs are absent then supply and demand do work in the usual way, and so they conclude that there are two different sets of labour market rules for two different sets of jobs and workers: one set of rules where there are ILMs and another set of rules where the laws of supply and demand apply. They try to convey this conclusion with their idea of a 'dual labour market'.

'Dual labour market' theory arises out of the radical economists' work on ILMs but it should not be understood as the same sort of concept. As Doeringer (1986) has latterly made clear, the term 'internal labour market' describes something that exists in practice: one sort of labour market territory in fact (see Chapter 1). The idea of a dual labour market (DLM) is not a new term for something which needs a name, but a metaphor which helps us to understand what goes on in real labour markets. In fact the metaphor helps us to understand (all sorts) of labour market territories, but readers should bear in mind that the DLM is a device and not a description.

DLM theory (see, for example, Gordon, 1972) noted the existence of labour market territories, particularly those associated with 'race', ethnicity and gender. It suggested that these territories could best be understood by economists if they started to think in terms of two sorts of employers, two sorts of workers, and two sorts of labour market.

'Primary' employers were those who used ILMs because they had expensive training investments (in workers) to protect. They paid the highest wages. 'Secondary' employers recruited on the open market and didn't worry about losing workers ('labour turnover'), probably because they didn't go in for much training. Employers might belong to the 'primary' or 'secondary' categories for a number of reasons, but 'primary' firms usually had more complex work processes, more sophisticated machines, and therefore greater skill requirements. Such firms would also add more value to their product and would in general make more profits as a result.

'Primary' workers were recruited by 'primary' employers, and 'secondary' workers were recruited by 'secondary' employers. The result was two separate labour markets – a 'primary' and a 'secondary' market – with an impermeable barrier between the two which neither workers (in search of jobs) nor employers (in search of workers) could penetrate.

If this was a bit strong, then perhaps the barrier was not completely impermeable and it might be more helpful to draw attention to the barrier itself rather than to the existence of separate labour markets – hence the term '*dual* labour market'. The DLM idea also served to remind people that this was an aid to understanding rather than a descriptive term. You could count far more than two labour markets if you set your mind to it (see Chapter 1), but the burden of the idea was not the number of labour markets but the existence of different types of labour market – one in which the laws of supply and demand could operate freely and another in which workers were insulated from competition by an ILM.

Even if these two types of labour market were used by the same firm (for recruitment to jobs with different sorts of machinery, for example), there would still be a barrier which workers crossed only with difficulty, but why should the barrier be associated with 'race', ethnicity or gender? The radical economists' explanation began, as before, with the institutions on the demand side of the labour market. They argued that employers did not see the labour of black and white workers, for example, as equivalent[4] and so might see whites as 'primary' workers whereas blacks were seen as 'secondary' workers.

As with simple ILM theory, DLM theory explains why the normal laws of supply and demand do not work in real labour markets. The DLM metaphor conveys the notion that barriers between or within labour markets prevent labour supply and demand adjusting towards an overall equilibrium point. All things are not equal and there is no free competition between all workers for all jobs. In consequence, wages in one type of labour market (the 'secondary' market) will remain much lower, and, furthermore, workers in such labour markets will not benefit from training and will have no career prospects.

At first glance it is not easy to see why the radical economists' ideas should prove any more attractive to sociologists than human capital theory, indeed sociologists in the United States have never been unreservedly enthusiastic about the work of these American economists. British sociologists, however, have been rather more keen on the ILM and DLM ideas despite the fact that the elaboration of the DLM theory (in the shape of a discussion of labour turnover) is as open to charges of 'blaming the victim' as human capital theory.

For example, DLM theory can be used to explain discrimination by institutions on the demand side of the labour market in terms of the supply side. As with human capital theory, it can be argued that the labour of blacks and whites (for instance) is not equivalent. It is not simply that blacks are less likely than whites to be picked for training by employers who have ILMs, black workers are different anyway and, therefore, have much less chance of entering an ILM.

It is probable that these apparent shortcomings were overlooked because the DLM idea drew attention – as the radical economists had hoped it would – to neglected areas of inequality in the labour market (like 'race' and gender) which were beginning to interest sociologists. At least in the early days, DLM theory was not thought to justify this inequality because it was, after all, the worst employers – the 'secondary' employers who paid low wages and so on – who were dispensable. They had little new technology, they added little value to their products, they did not even make profits. The economy, therefore, would not miss these 'exploiters of blacks and women' were they to disappear tomorrow.[5]

The second institutionalist theory can be described in fewer words. It has already been noted that this theory seeks to make basic economic theory fit the empirical evidence by attending to institutions on the supply side of the labour market, particularly to the role of labour unions. This approach is sometimes identified with the 'Austrian school' because the early exponents of this theory, notably Hayek, were Austrian economists; but elements of the theory have been popularised in the United States by Milton Friedman, and in the United Kingdom by Patrick Minford.

Minford (1985) argues that established industrial countries have social or legal arrangements (including the 'restrictive practices' mentioned in Chapter 1) which limit labour market competition between workers. These arrangements obstruct the operation of the laws of supply and demand and result in 'false' pricing. For example, it is argued that labour unions set wages at a higher level than would be dictated by the unobstructed operation of the laws of supply and demand. The unions prevent the proper operation of the laws of supply and demand because they set an artificial lower limit on the price of labour. Because wages cannot adjust below a certain level the supply of labour will exceed the demand and there will be unemployment.

A similar argument has been applied in respect of state welfare provision. The state's arrangements for social security for the unemployed dissuade people from applying for jobs which pay wages near the level of benefits. Minford and Peel are so sure of this that they find it amazing that a lot of people in lower-paid jobs choose to work at all:

It is probably habit, the desire to avoid upheaval, and the knowledge that the system must surely be changed in time, which prevent many more people from actually abandoning their existing jobs, rather than simply not making active efforts to find new ones.

(Minford and Peel, 1981, p. 6)

In any event, it is argued that welfare benefits prevent the adjustment of labour supply and demand through the price mechanism. Because they can claim welfare, people will remain unemployed while there are unfilled vacancies.

The theories of the Austrian school were never as popular with economists as they were with Western politicians and their advisers. The cause of this disagreement lies in the policy prescriptions which arise when the Austrian theory is applied to the macroeconomics of output and employment in a whole country. At this level, it has often been argued that wages are set too high (as a result of the supply-side institutional constraints on competition) and hence set limits on the growth of output and/or cause price inflation. A sensible government will therefore take steps to limit the wage-setting power of unions and reduce welfare benefits, and so allow free rein to the laws of supply and demand, or, as the politicians (most notably Reagan and Thatcher) once put it, 'allow the free play of market forces'.

From the foregoing, the reader may have guessed that the Austrian school is not very popular amongst sociologists. In general, all sociologists appear to be keener on the line of enquiry pursued by the radical economists, than on the Austrian approach, when pressed to choose between the two. The radical economists' theory does not suggest that limitations on competition are harmful and should be done away with. It identifies the source of these limitations in the practices of employers and argues, in effect, that employers must know what is best (for employers in a capitalist economy).

The Austrians, on the other hand, identified the source of limitations on competition on the supply side and argued that these were bad for employers, and (therefore) for everyone else. They have even suggested that the economic policy of all governments in capitalist countries can only be put on a sound footing by limiting the power of institutions to create 'imperfections' and 'distortions' in the labour market.

It would be foolish to be misled, however, into rejecting one or other of the institutionalist theories out of hand. We do not have to believe that employers know what they are doing, in order to recognise the importance of institutions on the demand side of the labour market. Similarly, we do not have to believe that unions or welfare benefits cause inflation, in order to take notice of the role of supply-side institutions in the workings of labour markets.

Individuals versus institutions?

If the foregoing constitutes a case for dismissing neither the radical nor Austrian approaches to institutionalist theories, a similar case can be made for taking the best of both the institutionalist theories and theories of human capital. At any rate, it would be unwise for sociologists to see these two types of theory as offering competing explanations.

In the first place, we have seen that the distinction between theories which make much of differences between individual workers, and those which begin by pointing to the role of institutions, sometimes breaks down. In the second place, is there really such a divide between a theory which says jobs and workers differ, and one which tells us there is no one, unified labour market? Both theories offer ways of describing limitations on competition, and both offer ways of explaining the observed lack of uniformity in labour market conditions. As has already been noted, both the individualist and institutionalist approaches have the same object in mind – to make *economic* theory a better fit with reality – and as far as sociologists are concerned many of the supposed differences between the two are not as fundamental as might be supposed on first acquaintance with the theories.

LABOUR MARKET SOCIOLOGY

It is clear from this brief discussion of economic theory that, when attempting to make their theories a better fit with the facts, economists could not avoid making their theories to some degree interdisciplinary. For example, if economists are trying to make their basic theory a more adequate explanation of real labour markets, they may quickly discover that real labour markets have physical territories (see Chapter 1). Once they attempt to build this geographical dimension into their theories, economists will take on some of the concerns of geographers. But it was not so much physical territories and the geographical dimension that concerned the economists discussed above, but social territories (for instance, occupational territories and 'race' and gender territories) and the sociological dimension. The economists found the limits of their original economic theory at the boundary between economic and social phenomena but pressed on to theorise the latter with the help of ideas like 'human capital' and 'dual labour markets'.

This explains why much of this work by economists has excited considerable interest amongst sociologists (for early examples see Jencks *et al.*, 1972; Barron and Norris, 1976), but this is not simply a case of sociologists blindly following the lead given by economists. In general, few sociologists have been interested in ideas of 'human capital' or 'dual labour markets' for the same reasons as economists. They have not been inspired by the economists' problem of making economic theory a better fit with the facts, but by sociologists' interest in social phenomena and theory.

To put it another way, economists might need to specify the 'tastes and preferences' which people hold in order to make their theory a better fit with reality, but they need not explain these tastes and preferences. For example, Becker, who did much to found the human capital approach, also attended to the empirical evidence of 'racial' discrimination. He assumed that people have a taste for discrimination (Becker, 1957). Employers, therefore, choose whether to satisfy this taste or not. If they do, they may incur costs, for example they may not hire the best worker for the job and/or they may have to pay higher wages. In the latter case there is a trade off between the satisfaction of tastes and the economic consequences of limiting competition between workers by discriminating against some of them (and effectively cutting down the supply of labour).

In Becker's analysis a taste (for discrimination) is specified but there is no explanation. We are none the wiser about why employers discriminate even though we know more about what happens when they do. Although questions about why people should have a taste for discrimination may be very important to some economists, they are not central to economic theory. Any further explanation is properly the province of another discipline – sociology, for example.

This chapter has supported the observation made in Chapter 1: that different disciplines have very different approaches to what appear to be the same subject matter. Every discipline therefore brings a unique approach – and not simply a different set of data – to the subject. Sociology does not simply bring its interest in social information but also sociological questions, and hopefully theory, to the study of labour markets. The following chapters will illustrate this point – a preview of the rest of the book is given at the end of this chapter – but the following brief example may give the reader a better idea of what sociology's unique approach entails.

Chapter 1 discussed the organisation of labour markets in terms of their regulation, particularly by states. In the following example of the sociological approach we will broaden the concept of organisation and begin to investigate exactly how the organisation of labour markets can be understood in relation to the abstract definition of labour markets given in Chapter 1.

All labour markets must be organised in some way. They do not appear spontaneously and even the 'hiring fair' discussed in Chapter 1 had to be organised (in this case, as a tradition). Most forms of organisation establish intermediaries between job-seekers and employers engaged in any of the five labour-market processes. An insight into the sociological approach can be gained from consideration of the role of intermediaries in just two of these processes – informing workers and informing employers.

The family is the subject of a vast sociological literature which has so much to say that labour markets usually only get a passing mention. Nevertheless, families are very important labour market intermediaries. Families frequently intervene in the process of informing employers where nepotism exists, and even where employers rely on informal recommendation ('putting in a good word') of new recruits.

From the job-seeker's point of view families are even more important. Not only may your family inform you about a particular vacancy, but your family can play a major part in informing you about what jobs are available to you in principle. In common with school and peer group, the family sets the norms and values which structure the process of informing workers – informing workers of where they will be able to get a job and whether that job will be suitable. For example, many parents have expectations (for example of upward social mobility) which lead them to direct their children towards particular jobs. Families can even inform potential job-seekers that there are no suitable vacancies for them. Thus girls have sometimes been discouraged from entering the labour market at all, or encouraged to leave the labour market after marriage or childbirth.

The fact that women, and rarely men, may either work part-time or not work at all after the birth of a first child is, once more, something which economic theory has no hope of explaining on its own. Because the family, and ideas about the family, are important, employers and job-seekers are informed (about potential recruits and potential vacancies) by the birth of a child (and sometimes even the prospect of parenthood). The questions which are raised are (social) questions of profound interest to sociologists.

This chapter has presented some sound reasons for believing that sociology is relevant to the study of labour markets. We already know (see Chapter 1) that sociologists have shown more and more interest in labour markets, but it should now be clear that there is a new, and exciting, possibility that that increased interest and proven relevance can be combined to the benefit of both sociology and the interdisciplinary study of labour markets. There is a unique opportunity, in other words, for sociology to be allowed into this area of study.

The interdisciplinary content of the new economic theories discussed above is only an example of something more general. While there are real labour market territories, we live in a world which also has *intellectual* territories: there are territories which define who has the right to speak and write about particular subjects. For example, many readers may have been unenthused by the title of this book. The term 'labour markets' will have suggested a variety of specialised (and probably impenetrable) language, bemusing graphs, and indigestible statistics. But, as a result of intellectual upheavals and social and economic changes (discussed in Chapter 1), it is now possible to open the area to wider debate, including debate within any social science (and between social sciences) that expresses an interest. Yet with this new opportunity comes a new danger.

THE STRUCTURE OF THIS BOOK

The opening up of debate on the subject of labour markets brings with it the temptation to organise the study of labour markets –

and hence the structure of this book – in terms of the intellectual upheavals or the social and economic changes which have created the opportunity. We might easily conceive, for example of a chapter (or two) on 'The arguments for and against labour market regulation', or one on 'The changing structure of labour supply'. In my view this would represent a waste of the new opportunity presented to sociology.

Similarly, I have taken the view that a textbook on the sociology of labour markets should not be structured according to the interests of economics (or any other disciplines). To have a chapter on human capital, another on dual labour markets and so on, would make it much more difficult to establish the *sociological* contribution to the interdisciplinary study of labour markets.

The structure of the book must derive from sociology, it should not be imposed from outside. Should it therefore be organised to reflect the interests of existing sociological sub-disciplines then: a chapter on gender and labour markets, the city and labour markets and so on? This might be an improvement but such a structure would suit a book on the subject of sociology *and* labour markets better than a book which is meant to be about the sociology *of* labour markets. To use the existing sub-disciplines of sociology to provide a structure would be to make the definition of a new sub-discipline – labour market sociology – that much more difficult. It would be much better to ask, instead, why the existing subdisciplines (and sociology as a whole) have shown an interest in labour markets.

There are particular sociological projects which are common to all sociologists and which lead them, in this instance, to the study of labour markets. The three most important projects are the investigation and theorisation of *society*, *economy* and *polity*. These projects can provide the foundations for a sociology of labour markets, and for this reason they will be used as organising principles for the rest of the book. Before the (simple) structure of the remaining chapters is explained, readers will require some description of the three projects and an explanation of the reason for sociological interest in each. This can be done in a simple way if we refer to the basic sociological concerns of social relations, social interaction and social groups.

At one level 'society' can mean everything, including economy and polity. For example, we have already considered differences between 'societies' which were really differences between countries or states or even collections of states. This is not the sense in which 'society' is used here. Instead, the term is meant to refer to those parts of our lives in which social considerations are uppermost. Such considerations arise from the pattern of social relations which are commonly understood in terms of social identities and divisions like family, community, gender, 'race' and class. These social relations find expression in social interaction and in the (formation and operation) of social groups – the family, after all, is the basic social group.

In those parts of our lives which we call economy, economic considerations are predominant. Whether we are taking part in exchange, production or consumption, economic calculations inform our activity. From the point of view of 'neo-classical' economics, such calculations are undertaken in order to minimise our costs and maximise our benefits, and these economists sum up this view of human behaviour in the term 'economic man'. But all economic activities may involve social interaction. Consider, for example, the different ways of conducting business in the United States, Japan and the Middle East. If there were no social interaction why would Western business-people think they required *social* training in order to do business in Tokyo and Riyadh? Similarly, there are economic institutions – firms and labour unions, for example – which are also, perforce, social groups. To illustrate this point, one need only think of the differences between firms and trade unions in the United States and Japan.

Since social interaction takes place in the economy, and social groups are formed there, economy is also of interest to sociologists and they should have something useful to say on the subject. To put it another way, there is a social dimension to all human behaviour.[6] Whereas much of economy can be understood in terms of the activity of 'economic men' (and women), this activity often has an important social dimension which can be investigated and theorised by sociologists.

Those parts of our lives which are labelled polity also have a social dimension. Students of politics are concerned with questions of power and authority, for example the powers exercised by governments. Political behaviour is to be understood in terms of the presence or absence of political power: do people have power, are they trying to get it, and what do they want to do with it? But just as there is more to economy than economics, so there is more to polity than politics.

Political behaviour also involves social interaction and political institutions are also social groups. Once more, a comparison between the United States and the Middle East provides an obvious example: political distinctions alone do not account for the differences in policy on discrimination in employment, for instance, between the United States and Middle Eastern states. Polity is not just reducible to the state, however, and further examples of the importance of social relations could be found in a comparison of political pressure groups in the United States and in the Middle East, or even in South Africa.

The remainder of this book is concerned with sociological work on society, economy and polity which can contribute to the study of labour markets by telling us more about the character of labour markets, their mode of operation, and about changes in labour markets. Chapter 3 is mostly to do with society, Chapter 4 is primarily concerned with economy, and most of Chapter 5 is about polity. The book ends with a concluding chapter which summarises the lessons of the preceding chapters and attempts to reach some conclusions about the theory and method of the sociology of labour markets.

SUMMARY

Whereas Chapter 1 showed that it was necessary to define the subject matter of the sociology of labour markets in order to decide what was relevant to this book, this chapter showed that we also needed to define the particular approach to the subject to which sociology, and no other social science, could lay claim. I took the view that this problem could be solved by contrasting the sociological approach with the one adopted by economists.

In very simple terms, economists are interested in labour markets because they are interested in all markets (as mechanisms for the distribution of resources through exchange). This is not the subject matter of the sociology of labour markets as defined in Chapter 1, but the interests of economists and sociologists coincide when economists try to make their abstract theories a better fit with what they know of real labour markets. Thus many economists have attended to the limitations on competition which mean the 'laws of supply and demand' do not work in the way that abstract theory says they should. In doing so, they have strayed onto common ground – common, that is, to sociologists as well as to economists.

The differences in subject matter (between sociology and economics) provide the first proof of the difference in approach. The unique approach of economists leads them to a particular type of theory, but application of the theory eventually leads economists towards problems which also interest sociologists. By contrasting the economists' and sociologists' treatment of these problems the sociological approach can be further illuminated. For example, economists are interested in labour market territories and boundaries because they seem to prevent the operation of the laws of supply and demand. Sociologists are interested in the same phenomena – the same evidence from real labour markets – because they seem to be caused (at least in part) by the social relations and processes that are the sociologists' stock-in-trade.

Economists may well be right to think that further efforts to understand 'tastes and preferences' are none of their concern, but such efforts are surely a necessary component of the interdisciplinary study of labour markets? If this is accepted, it is clear that sociology is well-placed to make a major contribution to this area of study.

Finally, this chapter explained that, in order to put the sociology of labour markets on a sound footing, the rest of the book would be organised according to the three sociological projects of society, economy and polity. We begin with society.

NOTES

1. Any choice of text will be arbitrary but readers might well begin with Fallon and Verry, 1988 or Sapsford, 1981.
2. This means you must spend less, and economists assume that we value

present consumption (the result of spending money now) more highly than future consumption.

3. There is evidence of differences in pay and employment patterns between blacks and whites which appear to be unrelated to any measurable difference in human capital. For example, throughout the 1980s the official United Kingdom Labour Force Survey showed that black unemployment rates were consistently higher than those of whites with the same qualifications.

4. Because of discrimination and/or for other reasons such as the assumed propensity of 'secondary' workers for higher labour turnover. Perhaps because they had learned the hard way after years of discrimination in recruitment and promotion, blacks – for instance – were thought to be less interested in staying with the same employer and so, the argument continued, employers did not bring blacks into ILMs because this would put their training investment at an unnecessary risk. It would simply be safer to hire, and train, white workers who would be much more amenable to a system which was, after all, *designed* to keep labour turnover to a minimum.

5. Latterly, Piore seems to have taken a different tack. He now appears to think that a new generation of 'secondary' employers may be good for everyone (see, for example, Piore and Sabel, 1984).

6. Just as there is an economic dimension: see, Becker, 1976.

3

PEOPLE AND WORK

In this chapter we first ask how sociologists' theories of society can help us to understand the origin and nature of labour markets. Whereas the second half of this chapter is concerned with more everyday matters related to the way in which the five labour market processes work, we begin with the way in which these labour market processes are established and their fundamental nature. This is really a very simple distinction to make. To take the labour market territories discussed in Chapter 1 as an example, in the current chapter we will, firstly, consider some explanations as to why such territories might exist in the first place; and, secondly, we will discuss the way in which people experience labour market territories.

SOCIETY AND THE PRINCIPLES OF LABOUR MARKETS

The explanations of the origin and nature of labour markets considered here give us some idea of the importance of two basic social principles in theorising labour markets. The first principle is the *social division of labour* in which different people do different things. The second principle is that of *social hierarchy* in which people and the things they do are ordered or ranked. These two social principles have interested sociologists for more than a century, and they might even be said to constitute the major preoccupations of the discipline, but their discussion in this book must be limited. We will deal only with what theories of the social division of labour and of social hierarchy can tell us of the origin and nature of labour markets.[1]

The social division of labour

In *The German Ideology*, Marx and Engels wrote of a utopian (communist) society in which:

nobody has one exclusive sphere of activity but each can become accomplished in any branch he wishes, society regulates the general production and thus makes it possible for me to do one thing today and another tomorrow, to hunt in the morning, fish in the afternoon, rear cattle in the evening, criticise after dinner, just as I have a mind, without ever becoming writer, fisherman, shepherd or critic.

(quoted by Rattansi, 1982, p. 12)

This vision could only be utopian, that is, a vision of a completely different sort of society, because we are all so accustomed to the social division of labour,[2] the principle that individuals don't do a *variety* of things. If labour is divided then different things are done by different people: writers write, fishers fish and so on. When a new form of labour comes into being a new class of people – to do this labour – comes with it. Furthermore, established types of labour are subdivided (the fisher no longer makes fishing nets) and people are subdivided along with the labour once more.

The social division of labour immediately poses one of the problems which the invention of labour markets ultimately solves and so provides us with a basic explanation of labour markets. If we all do the same thing we have no problem of distributing or allocating people to labours and labours to people since there is nothing to distribute. But as soon as we have different labours and differences between people then we have a problem: exactly *who* will do exactly *what*? This calls for rudimentary processes for informing, screening and offering labour.

Labour markets allocate different people to different sorts of labour (and vice-versa). There would be no need for labour markets were it not for the social division of labour in which different people do different things, but the idea of the social division of labour does not exhaust the contribution made by sociologists' theories of society to our understanding of the origin and nature of labour markets. For example, these theories can tell us rather more about how the idea of different people doing different things arises, and how it becomes accepted, becomes a legitimate social principle, thereafter.

In the first instance, we can turn to ideas which are closely associated with theories of the social division of labour, for example, ideas of *natural differences* and *specialisation*. Most early sociologists had an explanation as to why the process of dividing labour should begin but, for the sake of consistency, we will continue with Marx as our guide:

Within a family, and, after further development, within a tribe, there springs up naturally a division of labour caused by differences of sex and age, and therefore based on a purely physiological foundation.

(Marx, 1976, p. 471)

For our purposes it does not matter that Marx might have wished to modify the way in which 'family' and 'tribe' are treated here (see Engels' footnote to this passage), and the question of the authenticity of 'natural' differences in sex and age will be discussed below. What concerns us immediately is the simple observation that things to do (hunting, gathering, tending the fire) develop, and that different people become responsible for different things to do on the basis of physiological differences that make them suitable for, or capable of, some labours and not others.

Leaving aside the question of how real or important the physiological differences are, this theory does not explain all the modern complexity of divided labour or what produces this complexity – the *continued development* of the social division of labour. There is, indeed, more to the idea of a social division of labour than a mere description of society. The idea also involves a theory of social change. Most sociologists (following the founding fathers) believe that the social division of labour increases as time passes. Each new type of labour which comes into being and each further subdivision of existing labour adds to the development of the social division of labour. The social division of labour is part of the sociological explanation of the birth of civilisation and society and once it starts we might assume that it simply gathers pace and can then be held to explain much of the social change (anything from changes in the shape of the family to changes in crime and punishment) that subsequently occurs.

Even if we point to other sorts of natural differences – for example, Marx notes differences in climate and resources (you can't grow bananas if you live near the arctic circle and you can't fish if you live in a desert) – we still cannot explain change and complexity. In order to do this, we might turn to another related idea: when *specialisation* occurs different people are given different labours because practice makes perfect, that is, people will do things more efficiently if they specialise in them.

The idea of specialisation can explain the further and continued development of the division of labour (especially subdivision of existing labours) and can contribute to an explanation of the origin of the social division of labour along with the idea of a natural basis to dividing labour and people. Both ideas – natural differences as well as specialisation – are required because the idea of specialisation (practice makes perfect) suggests a reason to divide labour but no system for dividing people. It is clear that some people should specialise but who? Without an additional (to specialisation) explanation we simply draw lots to decide who does what.

We therefore return to the assumed natural differences between people which have already been offered as one explanation for the origin of the social division of labour. For example, in addition to the assumed differences in physical and mental ability between people of different ages and sexes, we can assume further differences in ability between individuals of the same age and sex. Further social division of labour – and all of the modern complexity which results – derives from the division of people according to ability to provide those who will undertake various specialised labours.

Ideas of natural differences and of specialisation add to our understanding of modern labour markets. For example, if we have a category of children's work we will need informing and screening procedures in order to decide when and on what basis any one thing to do fits into this category. Similarly we will need informing and screening procedures in order to decide when and on what basis any one individual fits into the category of child (cf. Aries, 1973). At the boundaries of either category – 'children's work' and 'child' – we may need some fairly complex procedures.

The idea of specialisation together with differences in ability between individuals suggests even more complex informing and screening procedures, and not just at the boundaries of categories. For example, is a particular labour going to be judged according to the strength required or the dexterity needed and how are these to be measured? Once the requirements of the labourer who is to specialise in this labour are established, then more informing and screening procedures are needed in order to establish whether an individual has the appropriate strength or dexterity for the task.

Many readers may not be wholly convinced by these arguments, however. The naturalistic explanation of the *origins* of the social division of labour can be challenged on the evidence (Berg, 1987). Certainly men cannot have babies and babies cannot throw spears, but aren't natural differences being given too much explanatory weight here? Unless we rely on the idea of specialisation, we have to assume that children naturally do one thing and not another: children's work is what children naturally do. If we do bring specialisation back into the argument we uncover another problem: why and how does specialisation start? Things happen because it would be useful if they did, but exactly how (and useful to *whom*) (see Rueschemeyer, 1986)?

Social hierarchy

Ideas of natural differences between people and of specialisation in different types of labour clearly help us to make the theory of a social division of labour a more adequate explanation of modern labour markets, but there is still something missing from our explanation. For example, how are 'natural' differences or the advantages of specialisation observed, how do they become important? The social division of labour is a funny thing to do (if you haven't done it already) and it doesn't make sense for people to start it (let alone pursue it) on what we have been given in the way of explanation so far.

The thing that is missing has apparently become such a familiar assumption that it is very hard to put one's finger on it (which may be part of the reason why Marx's utopian vision seems so desirable but also so unattainable). Nevertheless, we can begin to see some light if we start to think about why the notion of questioning the origins of the social division of labour is *not* something that usually occurs to us. In other words, what is it that stops us thinking of the social division of labour as a funny thing to do?

In practice the social division of labour involves qualitative differences between labours and between people. The evidence shows that it is not just different things and different people to do them, but things to do and people are seen as having different values. These are not values in the sense of each thing and person being valuable in itself or in different ways, but rather one thing or person is seen as more valuable than another. In other words, there is hierarchy.

The idea of social hierarchy is the second social principle of labour markets. According to this principle all (or most) of the things people do, and people themselves, can be evaluated according to general criteria. Some things and people will be of equivalent value but there will, necessarily, be a range of differences from the most to the least valuable. There will, therefore, be hierarchical grading.

Without the social principle of hierarchy the social division of labour can be no more than an abstraction. The idea of different people doing different things cannot be put into practice unless the people and things to do are seen as having different values. The development of labour markets therefore depends on the social acceptance and social construction of hierarchies (of people and of things to do). The principle of hierarchy is accepted when it becomes part of common sense, a tenet of religion, a scientific axiom and so on. Hierarchies are socially constructed in a variety of ways, according to age, according to gender, and according to many other criteria which will be considered at some length below.

Some sociologists simply accept the existence of social hierarchy as a self-evident truth, others see it – in turn – as something that requires explanation, but in either case it is social hierarchy that makes the social division of labour not such a funny thing to do. For example, if people believe in the existence or acceptability of social hierarchy in principle they will not find it hard to see (or *make* – by evaluation) qualitative differences between people and between labours and so accept, even demand, that different people should do different things. The belief in hierarchy leads to the acceptance of the idea that types of work and types of people are different, thus making the social division of labour – different people do different types of work – acceptable, even preferable (Durkheim, 1933).

Social groups, relations and institutions

How are the two social principles (of division of labour and of hierarchy) put into practice? Specifically, who makes these principles an important part of our social life: who makes them real for us, who carries the principles forward from one generation to the next? Sociologists find answers to these questions by way of ideas that lie at the heart of the discipline of sociology.

There is, firstly, a common sociological interest in social groups, social relations, and social institutions which are thought to constitute the warp and weft of the fabric of society. Readers will now be familiar with the most common examples of warp and weft: families, communities, nations, 'races', genders and classes. We might easily add relations between people with a disability and others, migrants and others, but in truth the list is endless.

Secondly, there are the key (sociological) explanatory concepts of *culture* and *power* which are used to explain both causes and effects of social groups, relations and institutions. For example, much sociological theory and research is concerned with how culture affects the behaviour of people and with how people wield power over others, and to what effect. In this view the social groups, relations and institutions discussed above can be seen as *locations* for both culture and power.

It would nevertheless be a mistake to organise the thoughts and findings of sociologists according to the headings of 'culture' and 'power' since the connection between the two is often intimate. A marginally better solution to the problem of organisation is the one adopted below. We will firstly consider three of the more common versions of an explanation (of the way in which the social division of labour and social hierarchy become social facts) which refers (for the most part) to things people do to themselves as a result of their membership of social groups, and the influence of social relations and institutions. We will then consider a second category of three explanations where sociologists have set more store by the things people do to other people as a result of their membership of social groups and so on.

We begin with *status attainment theory* (Blau and Duncan, 1969; Hauser and Featherman, 1977; Jencks *et al.*, 1972; Sewell and Hauser, 1975). In very simple terms, the theory of status attainment suggests that social hierarchy is largely a question of the status people eventually achieve in paid employment (measured at the highest point in their career, for instance). In large part this status represents a pay-off for earlier educational achievement. So far, this seems to recall the economists' theory of human capital (see Chapter 2), but status attainment theory also suggests that educational achievement is largely determined by family background (and perhaps the influence of 'significant others') which decides how much anyone wants out of education and, more importantly perhaps, how much they *can* get out of it. That is, family background determines (mental) ability. Having entered paid employment, the type of job acquired together with family background and educational attainment determine subsequent status.

Given the importance which status attainment theory assigns to family background, it is no surprise that the theory predicts that people (or, at least, sons) will end up with a status not too dissimilar to that of their parents (or, rather, their fathers). 'Short social mobility' is of course characteristic of many people in advanced industrial societies, but status attainment theory does not offer the only plausible explanation as to why sons should end up with a similar status to their fathers. It is a central proposition of status attainment theory that people are in general agreement about the criteria on which social hierarchy is based and about the position of individuals in that hierarchy (Jencks *et al.*, 1972, p. 177; Hauser and Featherman, 1977, p. 8). There are, however, other explanations of short social mobility which do *not* rely on the assumption of a generally-agreed hierarchy.

Firstly, there are theories (see, Moynihan, 1969; for criticism see Miller, 1981) which address *the relationship between culture and poverty*. Such theories suggest that particular cultures or 'subcultures' (of the poor, of particular ethnicities, of particular social classes, for example) lower both expectations and achievement levels. It is argued that some people are so culturally handicapped as to be unable to take advantage of education and training that might raise their status. The poor therefore stay poor and the deprived stay deprived.

The final variation on the theme of what people do to themselves as a result of their membership of social groups and the influence of social relations and institutions pushes this logic a stage further. In the literature on attitudes and *orientations* there is very little mention of an agreed hierarchy or of cultural handicap. Instead, it is assumed that a variety of different categories of people have their own, peculiar social hierarchies against which success or failure can be measured.

Sociologists who use the idea of different orientations have not limited themselves to the consideration of what people think about paid employment (Parsons and Shils, 1951; Weber, 1964). Indeed, the best-known example of the application of the idea in Britain was concerned with peoples' orientations *away* from paid employment (Goldthorpe *et al.*, 1968; see also Scase and Goffee, 1989). When applied to peoples' labour market experiences, however, the idea of differences in orientations produces a simple conclusion: people have different measures (according to their class, their age and so on) for deciding whether something (a level of educational attainment or a particular job) fits the bill or not. There is no universal measure for deciding what one's goal is or for judging whether a goal has been achieved, rather people (in groups) construct their own measures.

The central theme of differences in orientations to paid employment has been reworked in several ways. Following the influential work of Ashton in the early 1970s (for a review, see Brown, 1982), some sociologists have concluded that differential access to education does not simply produce different qualifications but also different orientations to employment (see Brown, 1987; Roberts, 1975; Williams, 1974; Willis, 1977). Others have been at pains to point out that the idea of orientation to a career makes sense to the working class although in rather different terms to the way in which the middle class think of a career (Brown, 1982) and have noted that orientations can be subject to complex influences, including the nature of the first job entered (Ashton *et al.*, 1990; Stewart *et al.*, 1980).

In more general terms, Coxon and Jones (1978) suggest that occupational 'images' differ from group to group, and argue that there is little point in producing a rank-order of occupations that cuts across these groups. They conclude that completely different hierarchies (of occupations) arise depending on which class one is investigating (Coxon and Jones, 1979). A similar conclusion is reached by Blackburn and Mann (1979; also see Sabel, 1982): for example, Blackburn and Mann document the way in which different people can come to vastly different conclusions on the basis on the same piece of information about a job (for instance, whether it involves manual or non-manual work, work indoors or outdoors). Both they and Sabel wonder, in fact, whether the whole idea of a hierarchy based on skill is a peculiarly middle-class perception.

In most of the foregoing, sociologists have used the idea of orientations to illuminate differences in attitudes towards occupations between social classes, but similar work has been done in respect of age groups (see Roberts *et al.*, 1984) and ethnic minorities (see especially, Bonacich, 1972, 1976; for a critical review of such work see Fevre, 1984; and for empirical criticism see Miller, 1981). But whatever the substantive focus of their research, researchers are usually agreed that families play some sort of role in producing and reproducing orientations to paid employment. This is particularly evident in work on differences in orientations relating to gender where the important family members are less likely to be the parents of people in the labour market than their own spouses and children.

Dex (1987) has shown that British women change the industries in which they work (and suffer downward social mobility as a result) over childbirth. This is in part a result of change in orientations arising from the demands of child-rearing. Before childbirth women are more concerned with occupational preferences but after childbirth finding a job with suitable hours of work becomes more important. Indeed, the recent expansion of part-time work in the United Kingdom has relied heavily on women workers who work part-time because this arrangement allows them to combine paid employment with the work of child-care (although note that the numbers of women returning as full-timers doubled during the 1980s – McRae and Daniel, 1991).

Dex's work is a good example of the difficulty of keeping particular types of research in watertight compartments. Crompton and Sanderson (1990) wonder how much of what Dex describes can really be seen as the result of free choices made by women. It is certainly not clear whether this and similar research automatically supports the idea that what people do to themselves is more important – as far as labour markets are concerned – than what other people do to them. This is a point which is made in a different way by other writers. Several of the authors considering the question of occupational choice in the collection of papers edited by Williams (1974) conclude that people's orientations are important enough, but that there is a great deal of evidence to suggest that people aim higher than the level they are likely to achieve, that they often have a fairly negative view of their *realistic* choices, and that occupational choice is, in reality, limited. Blackburn and Mann (1979) and Ashton *et al.* (1990) agree that while people may have all sorts of different attitudes to work they end up having to settle for what is available. 'What is available' is influenced, in part, by the things people do to other people as a result of their membership of social groups and so on, and it is to three examples of theories which are primarily concerned with what some people do to other people that we turn next.

We begin with a fairly weak version of this argument, one that is not always confident about the primacy of what some people do to others: one sort of theory of the importance of *social networks* (see Granovetter, 1973, 1974; Grieco, 1987; Harris *et al.*, 1987; Harris and Lee, 1988; Windolf and Wood, 1988). In simple terms, it is argued that the sort of social networks an individual has or does not have will play a major role in determining the sort of job (or type of unemployment) they end up in. Social networks can provide both information about jobs and may even help job-seekers to secure jobs when they already know a position is vacant. Job-seekers are therefore, in a sense, at the mercy (or at least in debt to) other members of their social networks, while job-seekers with poor networks, or none at all, find their own opportunities limited by the actions of others.

It is possible (Fevre, 1989a) to describe the effect of social networks in terms of the second version of a theory which gives primacy to what some people do to others – Weber's theory of *social closure*. Unlike another theory of 'closure' considered in the next chapter, Weber's theory concerns peoples' efforts to win a competition and not their efforts to avoid competing at all. The idea of social closure arises from Weber's (1964, 1968) interest in how people try to hold on to or increase their power over others and their advantages over others (including their control over resources, for example wealth – also see Halsey, 1981). Weber's best-known statement of the theory of social closure (Weber,

1968, p. 342) has inspired several sociologists (see, for example, Kreckel, 1980) to see social closure as the basis of the sociology of labour markets.

This view is expressed at length by Parkin who writes that, for Weber, social closure 'means the process by which social collectivities seek to maximize rewards by restricting access to a limited circle of eligibles' (Parkin, 1979, p. 44). In the labour market, then, groups of workers will seek to monopolise particular jobs. By manipulation of credentials or other eligibility criteria such as membership of particular labour unions or professional associations, they will close off some employment opportunities, and may even seek to control recruitment directly. Parkin goes on (1979, pp. 44–116) to describe social closure as 'exclusion' (individualist and collectivist), 'usurpation' (what outsiders do when collectively excluded), and 'dual closure' (which occurs, for example, when workers are trying to usurp employers and the state but are also attempting to exclude other workers).

The final example of a theory which explains how the social division of labour and social hierarchy become facts by reference to what some people do to others rests its case on the issue of *domination*. There is, for example, research by feminists and others which describes the way in which male trade unionists close off employment opportunities to women in an effort to maintain male domination. Other theories suggest that labour markets *per se* are made to work in a way which preserves the unequal power relationships characteristic of 'patriarchal domination' (for general discussion of male domination see Delphy, 1977; Millett, 1977; Walby, 1986; for a general discussion of patriarchy, see Bradley, 1989). Similar work has been done in respect of 'racial domination' (Blauner, 1972; Baron, 1975) and 'institutional racism' (Carmichael and Hamilton, 1968; Sivanandan, 1982).

Social values

With the addition of the second social principle of hierarchy we can be much happier that we have a good idea of how what sociologists say about society can help us to understand the origin and nature of labour markets. In particular we can be much happier about the explanation of the origin of rudimentary labour market processes given above, but for us to improve the explanation to the point at which we can explain more than the rudiments of labour markets, we need to know a bit more about social hierarchy. Most obviously, we need to know what hierarchy is based on – what are the general criteria that are applied to people and labours? Finding answers to these questions will help us to explain further the origins and, especially, the nature of labour markets. Sociologists have provided a number of answers and the most important ones will be considered below.[3]

Although 'hybrid' explanations are common, the criteria which sociologists identify as the basis of social hierarchy fall into three categories. There are those sociologists who say that hierarchy is based on people, those who say it is based on labour or work, and those who argue that hierarchy is based on the labour market itself. If the explanation of the workings of labour markets is based on differences between people, then (for the most part), hierarchical criteria will be 'people-based' and the value of labours will be derived from the people who perform them. If the explanation is based on differences between types of work, then it is in work that the criteria on which any hierarchy is based can be found. Finally, if we consider that the labour market is the basis of hierarchy then the criteria for the hierarchies of work *and* the people who perform work will be found there, in the market.

Differences between people are the source of social hierarchy
The general idea of this sort of theory is that what the labour market does, what it cannot *avoid* doing, is reflecting the fact that people are the basis of all hierarchy. The labour market reflects this principle so far as labour is concerned and will therefore be made to work in a particular way (simply) in order to reproduce this principle. This explains both the origin and nature of the five labour market processes: it is what they are (allowed to be) for. If people are the source of the hierarchical principle, then people are judged according to who they are, and work according to whose work it is.

If you say the source of hierarchical criteria is differences between people, then you must find something in the people that can be a general source of social hierarchy, not simply of criteria used in the labour market. There are, in fact, many different criteria, as many different types as there are different ways of classifying people. For example, people can be classified according to their religion. Thus O'Dowd *et al.* (1980) and Jenkins (1988) say that society in Northern Ireland is stratified by religious affiliation and that the labour market there operates to reproduce this stratification with Catholics ending up in the worst work or in no work at all.

To see how labour market processes operate according to this view let us take a rather more common example of an argument which says differences between people are the basis of hierarchy: a particular sort of feminist theory of gender and the labour market (for overviews of gender and labour market theories, see, for example, Beechey, 1987; Bradley, 1989; Dex, 1985; Walby, 1988). This theory holds that real (sex) differences are not what matter but the social (gender) differences that are created between men and women. But, on the basis of this socially constructed difference, a social hierarchy ('patriarchy') is constructed. As a result, everything in society may reflect and reproduce the hierarchy – everything, for example, is *gendered*. Genders are assigned to people and so people are given values, and so are categories of work given genders and therefore values (see, for example, Curran, 1988). For instance, according to *Social Trends*, in the United Kingdom in 1989 73 per cent of men and 62 per cent of women thought a car mechanic's job was only suitable for men. Nearly 60 per cent of men and half of the women surveyed thought a secretary's job was only suitable for women.[4] Not only is there some work which is male and other work which is female, but being in paid employment *at all* can be more male than female.

Male is seen as better than female, whether it is people, conversation or work. People's gender is the ultimate measure of value: both of paid employment versus other labour (like housework) and of any work that is ever created. Since gender is the source of value, being in work or not and the particular work you are in derives its value from the gender-status of the work. At the most simple level, the labour market operates to make sure that the genders of people and the genders of their work are the same. In this way the hierarchy is reflected but also reproduced:

the values given to people and to work are maintained and (through differences in pay and so on) the rest of the social hierarchy is reproduced as well. What are the five labour market processes doing according to this view? The five processes now have some basis for distributing people and work, for example women are channelled into women's work such as unpaid domestic labour, paid domestic labour, caring and feminine professions.

The feminist theory of gender and labour markets has only been an example of a theory which says people are used as the basis of the values that come from and reproduce social hierarchy. We might have rehearsed the same arguments for theories of 'race' (Baron, 1975; Jenkins, 1986) and theories of 'stages of the life cycle' (cf. Ashton *et al.*, 1990). For example, we might have discussed the idea that there is a social hierarchy based on 'race' and that labour markets then operate to reproduce that hierarchy. People do or do not get work at all, and get a particular type of work, because this type of work is assigned to a 'race'. In consequence, blacks (and the young and the old) are distributed to some types of work and not others, or are not included in paid work at all.

To conclude, I will say a little about how this type of theory manages to explain *change* without violating the basic assumptions of the theory. This can be done in a variety of ways, for example, we may argue that change in labour markets results from shifts from one sort of people-based criterion to another: gender may cease to matter (as a result of political challenge to the social hierarchy) but another people-based category like the stages of the life-cycle may come to matter more. Similarly, there may be battles over whether, where and how the people-based criterion should matter. There is also the possibility of battles over what person-value a particular type of work (or work as a whole) has. For example, the debates which preceded the passing of the Factory Acts in Britain made people wonder whether a type of work (chimney sweeping or coal mining) was children's work, and, ultimately, whether any paid employment was work for children (similarly for women) (Bradley, 1989; Driver, 1970; Fyfe, 1989; Pinchbeck, 1981; Wing 1967). In passing we might note that these struggles did not alter the fact that stages of the life cycle formed the basis of a social hierarchy (consider, for example, the nature of the various arguments used to persuade people of the moral rectitude of limiting child labour).

Differences between types of work are the basis of social hierarchy

If differences between types of work are seen as the basis of hierarchy, the argument is the same as before, only in reverse. It is argued that work is the source of hierarchical criteria and that the labour market criteria for people therefore refer to what they can do, whereas for work the criteria arise from what the work is said to require of the person who does it.

Readers may know that there is a structural-functionalist school in sociology and that a variety of different views come under the broad heading of structural-functionalism. But if we were to reduce the structural-functionalist approach to a simple formula (perhaps too simple for any structural-functionalist writer to approve), we would say, firstly, that structural-functionalism sees stratification as useful or necessary to society (Parsons, 1951; Parsons and Shils, 1951). Secondly, structural-functionalist theory finds the basis of social stratification in 'role' or 'function' (Tumin, 1967, p. 10). In simple terms, one's place in the hierarchy is determined by one's usefulness to society and all of social hierarchy arises from the difference in value of the contributions that various people make to society. It is easy to see how this assumption translates into an analysis of labour market hierarchies (and hence processes): what one does at work allows an easy measure of usefulness or function in an industrial society. But exactly what are the differences in work to which different values are attached?

Firstly, working (not necessarily in paid employment) has more value than not working, not working is not fulfilling any role or function and so may have no value at all. People who do not work are therefore at the bottom of the social hierarchy. Secondly, work is created as 'qualitatively different role specialisations' (Smelser, 1963, p. 14). Value comes from the differences which are created in the nature of the role, for example whether it requires work by hand or by brain. Just as in the previous section, where male had more value than female, so here work by brain has more value than work by hand.

This is not to say, however, that feminist and structural-functionalist theories can easily be reconciled. A major point of disagreement lies in the feminist belief that a statement about the different values attached to male and female things is a statement of fact, but a statement of facts that should nevertheless be changed. On the whole, structural-functionalists think qualitative role specialisations are a good idea and believe that the way values are attached to different forms of work should not be changed.

In fact (as we will see below) the two views do have something else in common. Both agree that 'fair', for example meritocratic, labour markets are best. This is, after all, what feminists are fighting for: the treatment of women on merit. The source of disagreement is a dispute about what the facts are. For the most part, structural-functionalists think we have that meritocracy (Parsons, 1964, p. 82) while feminists say we do not have it yet. The question of whether it is possible, or appropriate, to judge these two opinions against empirical evidence will be discussed below, but for the moment, at least, we are not concerned with how labour markets should happen but with how labour markets do happen.

Structural-functionalists conclude that the (five) labour market processes exist in order to allocate the right people to appropriate work according to values which derive from differences between different types of work. But how are these values attached to people? People are evaluated according to their capacity or ability. If they are capable of no work they have no value. If they are capable of highly skilled mental work they have high value. Labour market processes therefore operate (as far as the supply side is concerned) to distribute individuals to appropriate work according to their capacities or abilities. Some theorists appear to believe that differences in capacity and ability occur naturally and that what the labour market does, in consequence, is to distribute people on the basis of the presence or absence of natural talents. This is certainly a part of the argument advanced by Davis and Moore (1945), but it is by no means necessary to the basic theory. We can assume, instead, that these differences in capacity derive wholly from differences in education and training.

A theory which finds the basis of social hierarchy in values derived from work can quite easily accommodate change. There may be change in the basis of the hierarchy (while remaining

work-based): for example manual skill may decrease in importance while computer literacy (a mental skill) assumes a new
importance. Secondly, there may be change which keeps the
hierarchy intact even while types of work such as unskilled
labouring disappear (rather like some child labour did in the
previous section). In both cases the motor for change is not
political struggle but technological change and changes in
education and training.

Labour markets are the basis of social hierarchy

According to Weberian sociologists, markets are the source of all
social hierarchy. This applies to other markets than the labour
market (see Rex and Moore, 1967 on the housing market), but the
labour market is nevertheless vitally important to social stratification in industrial society. As we will see below, whether you are
in the labour market or not is fundamental to your place in society
and it is in the labour market that all the gradations of social class
are initially produced.

There may be 'real' differences between types of work and
between people but as far as the labour market is concerned these
do not matter. What matter are the differences between types of
work and between people that labour markets create and, in the
Weberian view, it is actually these market-based differences that
the theories discussed in the preceding two sections have really
been trying to explain (at least so far as they were concerned with
industrial societies) rather than with hypothesised 'real' differences
that may or may not exist.

The basis of value in this schema has already been described in
Chapter 2: it is relative scarcity. People whose labour is in greater
demand have a higher value and work which is in greater demand
amongst those seeking work has a greater value. To repeat the
warning of Chapter 2, the emphasis is on relative scarcity rather
than absolute volume of work or workers. Thus those workers for
whom there is a tighter labour market (and not those for whom
there is the greatest volume of work) will have a higher value.
Similarly, those types of work for which the demand for work
tends to exceed the supply of work will also have a greater value.

In practice, this theory is usually applied to the workers alone.
Ideas of 'market situation', and 'market capacity' are used to

convey the idea that the market itself is the source of the value of the people. Weber writes that:

By the 'market situation' (*marktage*) for any object of exchange is meant all the opportunities for exchanging it for money which are known by the participants in the market situation to be available to them and relevant in orientating their attitudes to prices and competition.

(Weber, 1964, pp. 181–2; also see Weber, 1968, pp. 82–6)

This idea became very popular with British sociologists like Giddens (1981, see also Lockwood, 1958) who defined *market capacity* as 'all forms of relevant attributes which individuals may bring to the bargaining encounter' (Giddens, 1981, p. 103). Market situation (see also Kreckel, 1980) is not directly related to who a person is or what they can do, but simply arises from how the market rates their market capacity – are they in demand or not and is there a sufficient supply of these workers or not? But even though this is rarely done, we could repeat the analysis for work too, for example we would assume that types of work are not rated according to whose work it is or what the work requires but according to how it is rated by the market.

So, it is neither the division of work nor of people that provides the basis of value and social hierarchy. The market is a law unto itself which bears little relation to work or people. It is the market itself that divides people, but how? On the basis of our market capacity, or, in other words, by reading the signs we bring to the labour market (and the signs different types of work bring to the labour market) which are interpreted and effected by the five labour market processes, and which determine the market situation of any type of work or person.

We already know what these signs are. In respect of people, evidence of education and training are signs that will be interpreted to establish market capacity (and therefore, market situation) and hence the possibilities of suitable work or any work at all. For work there are signs like 'work requirements' and 'women's work' as well as evidence of pay and conditions. But the reader must understand that all of these are signs only. They are not real, but the way in which the labour market works – that is, they are located in the market (to be precise, in the five processes) and not outside (in people or in work).

It is very important at this point to clarify the distinction between this view and the structural-functionalist approach. In the latter abilities are unevenly distributed across the population; different work requires different abilities; the labour market distributes the right people to the right work. In the Weberian view there need not be an uneven distribution of real abilities (we can remain agnostic on this) but simply an uneven distribution of the things (completed apprenticeships, qualifications and so on) which are commonly believed to be signs of such abilities. Similarly, different types of work in the labour market need not require different abilities but are divided according to signs (like pay) which suggest that they are. Employers and workers use these signs to distribute people to work.

So, for example, similarly skilled people are distributed to work which might actually require some skill but are distributed on the basis of employers' belief in the differences in skill required in each type of work, and the differences in people's skills as signified by their possession of educational qualifications, but this is as much as we can say. For example, let us assume that much of the better paying work in the Civil Service requires a demonstration of knowledge of statistics. Once in this work, not even basic numeracy, let alone a knowledge of statistics, may actually be required. Nevertheless, absence or presence of statistical training is used to distribute workers to work (it is said to be a requirement of *both*).

So, according to this view, what is the origin and nature of the five labour market processes? The labour market processes (information, screening, offers) are the means by which it is simultaneously decided that any particular type of work and any particular person have a certain value. Labour market processes (then) distribute workers to work of the same value, but what about the people who do not make it to the labour market at all, or are altogether unsuccessful in their labour market activity?

In the previous two sections those lower down a social hierarchy were more likely to lose out (for example, on the basis of gendered paid employment women are last hired and first fired), but here the source of social hierarchy is the labour market itself so how can labour market processes operate in this way? People who lose out do so simply because the market doesn't want them, but why doesn't it want women, or unskilled men, for example? In the terms of the Weberian theory, this is no more a question that we need to ask than were questions such as 'why is work gendered?' or 'why is manual work low-value work?' in the preceding sections. It is simply the case that women and unskilled workers have no market capacity to speak of and so do not find work. The idea of having no value in the hierarchy is conveyed by Giddens (1981) with the notion of 'underclass', but many other sociologists have described how the unemployed fall out of the working class, or out of the social structure (Goldthorpe and Payne, 1986; Harris *et al.*, 1987). Once more, we could repeat the analysis as far as work is concerned. Some work is so unpopular (for example, because wages are too low, or because conditions are intolerable) that no worker wants to do it.

Before we conclude this section, one important point of difference between the Weberian view and the view discussed in the previous section must be stressed. Structural-functionalists have, on occasion, argued that Weber thought labour markets became such an important source of hierarchy because it was self-evident that they represent a 'better' or 'fairer' way of doing things. Arguably, this wasn't what Weber intended at all (Albrow, 1970): he thought that labour markets became accepted as a legitimate basis for (reproduction of) hierarchy because of a change in the way people think which makes them see markets as 'better' or 'fairer'.[5]

This clarification removes an obstacle to our full understanding of ideas of market situation and capacity. Weberian theory requires that people have accepted a particular view of the world before labour markets can develop fully. They must accept they are represented by the signs they bring to the labour market and agree to take the verdict of the market on the chin; employers have to agree all this (is sensible) too. This acceptance comes when people are generally persuaded that criteria which are rational, legal and universal offer the best basis for doing (such) things. It was the change towards this type of thinking (especially in relation to markets – and especially labour markets) that Weber was trying to point out.

There is therefore a further crucial difference between this approach and the approaches discussed in the previous two sections. Whereas both the feminist and structural-functionalist examples, in their different ways, did not shrink from value-judgements (about what should or should not be the nature of the labour market), this Weberian theory (as we might expect) attempts to stand outside such debates. Instead of saying this should or should not be, Weberian theory simply says this is how people *see things* – as legitimate or not, as should or should not be.

Finally, as in the preceding sections, we must say a word or two on change. In the Weberian view, once the market has been accepted as the maker of values then change becomes simply a matter of change in the market. That is, it is change in relative scarcity (values) that matters, as a result, for example, of change in education and training (increased certification for instance, as described by Ashton, 1988a; Ashton *et al.*, 1990; Windolf and Wood, 1988); and changes in technology or in industrial structure (see Windolf and Wood, 1988, especially pp. 163-98, who introduce international comparisons into their discussion of such changes). In Britain, for example, Goldthorpe (1982, 1987) has documented the growth of the service *sector* and the rise of the 'service *class*'.

SOCIETY AND THE WORKINGS OF LABOUR MARKETS

People choose the sort of job they want using all sorts of criteria: where it is, how much the pay is, whether it will be nice to do, whether they like the people working there already and so on. But people do not often get exactly the job they want: they have to choose one of the jobs (if there are any) that employers are prepared to entertain them for. There may be difficulties in finding out about such jobs and sometimes we need other people to help us find out about them, to tell us whether there is a job at all, and to help us to decide whether it is one we want.

But even if a person finds out about a vacant job that they want, this does not mean that they will get that job. The employer has to decide whether they want one person or another. How they decide this can be very complicated. Most employers want to know whether applicants will be able to do the job, or even if they will be able to do it better than anyone else (who wants it). They try to find this out in all sorts of ways but they have at least as many problems in finding out about people as people do in finding out about jobs.

Employers can never be sure that everyone who would like the job has heard about it and they may have a terrible time trying to decide who is best for the job when there are lots of applicants. Usually they cannot decide what 'best' for the job means, let alone how to decide who is best. For example, what information should count in their decision: how applicants look, how they behave, who they know; documentary evidence, non-documentary evidence; and how does the employer gather all this information? Hudson and Sadler refer to a case in which 3,500 people were interviewed for twenty-four vacancies; and the successful candidates 'were interviewed up to six times at various hours of the day and night' (Hudson and Sadler, 1989, p. 118; see also Catt, 1984). Often employers have other things on their minds anyway, like who deserves the job, being nice to people they like, returning favours and that sort of thing. Some employers just give up on trying to find the best person altogether or let other people choose for them (Fevre, 1989a).

Readers will have realised that we have just reviewed once more the processes of finding work and finding workers while again neglecting to mention the parallel processes of leaving work and getting rid of workers. But readers can easily see for themselves that voluntary quits and firing (dismissals and redundancies) involve just as much complexity as hiring. Readers may also conclude that both hiring and firing seem to reserve a place of honour for luck.

It seems to be a matter of luck which jobs people end up with and which workers employers end up with. This was certainly the impression given by Thomas Hardy when he described the hearty labourers 'waiting upon Chance' (see p. 10 above) and Marx seems to have shared this view. Because labour is treated like a commodity 'and it is a bit of luck for him if he can find a buyer' (*Economic and Philosophic Manuscripts of 1844*), the labourer is alienated:

Estrangement is manifested not only in the fact that my means of life belong to someone else, but also in the fact that . . . all is under the sway of inhuman power [i.e. the labour market].
(Quoted by Rattansi, 1982, p. 16)

Contemporary sociologists (for example Harris *et al.*, 1987) who have tried to look at this from the job-seeker's point of view, to predict what job a worker will get (or even if they will get a job at all), have not been wholly successful (Mackay, 1988), but we would still be wrong to reduce the workings of labour markets to chance.

We know (from Chapter 1) that if we take a step back to look at the aggregate picture, we will find patterns, and we already know something about some of these patterns. If we look at the labour market experience of workers, for example, we can find patterns associated with gender, stage of the life cycle, 'race', type of family or social network, type of community, social background, level of education and training and so on.

For example, there are labour market patterns ('destinations') which seem to reflect social background ('origins') (cf. Halsey *et al.*, 1980), and Goldthorpe and Payne (1986) point out that there has been little underlying change in such patterns of social mobility in the United Kingdom (that cannot be explained by changes in labour market opportunities). Similarly, there are general patterns in the labour market experiences of black workers. For many years black workers in the United Kingdom had low unemployment rates but tended to occupy the jobs that other workers did not want. In the 1980s a new pattern emerged: black workers had higher unemployment than the workforce in general but those who remained in work tended to occupy better jobs than before (Barber, 1985; Brown, 1984; OPCS, 1987, 1989a).

It may all look like luck when we get down to the nitty-gritty of labour market *workings*, but if we step back we can see the proof of the values we discussed earlier in this chapter in the shape of real labour market patterns. So how does this happen – what do sociologists who write about society have to say about how labour markets work?

We understand the social origins of labour markets in terms of a combination of the division of labour and of hierarchy. But there are 'alternative' versions of this combination which produce three different views of the fundamental nature of labour markets. Now these three views also offer us our first set of answers to one of the questions that illuminates the workings of labour markets. If your view of the origins and nature of labour markets makes much of the importance of 'people values' then you will think this is how the labour market works; similarly, you may think that labour markets work according to 'work values' or 'market values'. We will now investigate exactly how each view of the origins and nature of labour markets translates into a view – or set of views – on how labour markets work.

Discrimination

The following discussion relies heavily, if not always uncritically, on Jewson and Mason (1986; see also Jenkins, 1988). In it we consider the idea that what is really going on in labour markets is that workers are being judged as good or bad people – that is, there is *discrimination* between people (and perhaps there are also related phenomena like favouritism and patronage). It can be argued that labour market patterns show the outcome of this discrimination: this is why blacks and women are in undesirable jobs or no jobs at all (see, for example, Marshall, 1974). This is, after all, how we would expect a labour market to work if we believed its fundamental nature (even its origins) to be best understood as based on the attachment of different values to people. What everyone does (or, at least, what is done by everyone who matters, for example employers) can be understood in these terms, but if there is anything that really does not fit the pattern (and this is often in dispute, for example are *more* jobs for women outside the pattern or does it have to be *better* jobs?) then this might indicate some movement towards merit in the labour market.

An example of such an explanation of the workings of labour markets might be research on social networks from which it is concluded that networks are concerned to distribute people on the basis of people-based judgements: networks make sure people-based values are what count (they are for 'looking after your own'). Or we might instance other theories, for example feminist theories which say that 'skill' is not real but simply a way of covering up for, or permitting, the judgement of people (see Coyle, 1982; Craig *et al.*, 1982; Game and Pringle, 1983; Phillips and Taylor, 1980).

At the extreme, we might attempt to explain everything about how the labour market works in terms of the evaluation of

people: everything is discrimination. This might be the result, for
example, where sociologists are deeply committed to the removal
of all forms of discrimination. There is certainly something in the
language of much of the literature (including Fevre, 1984) which
suggests many sociologists run serious risks of misrepresentation
when they write on this topic. People who believe that
discrimination is more-or-less characteristic of labour markets
tend also to believe that people-based values are bad. This may
not always seem obvious at first glance, but it is evident in the
pejorative terms which are sometimes used (and sometimes
selectively used) to describe the operation of labour market
processes. This sort of view has been largely responsible for the
popular association of 'discrimination' with 'bad' but rarely
discusses discrimination (between jobs) by employees. In related
discussion of patronage there is frequent use of terms like
'favouritism', 'blue-eyed boy', 'jobs for the boys' and 'old school
tie'. All of these terms imply unfairness or cheating, and they do
so because the way things are interpreted to be is being (implicitly)
compared to the way things ought to work (if they were fair).

Selection

Secondly, there is the idea (see Tumin, 1967) that what is really
going on in labour markets is that employers are getting the best
people for different types of work. Everything in the variety of
labour market patterns is thought to reflect this, while everything
employers do and everything job-seekers do is done with this in
mind. Davis and Moore (1945) describe the different social
positions and the need to allocate people to these positions which
are each of different value to society. Social inequality is the
mechanism by which the positions are filled, although rank is not
just decided by functional importance since the ease of filling
vacancies competently is also considered. In any event, some
sociologists see selection as *the* way in which labour markets
work:

Universalism and functional specificity are much more readily recog-
nizable as pattern principles underlying specific institutional forms. The

first is particularly important in two fields, the patterns governing personal status and rights, and those governing the treatment of ability and achievement. The principal freedoms which we have come to value so highly, and the relative immunity from invidious discriminations on such grounds as birth, individual favouritisms, ethnic or class status, have their roots in this pattern. 'Equality before the law' is doubtless very far from being able to guarantee effective substantive equality for 'all sorts and conditions of men', but that kind of particularistic discrimination is surely far less prominent in our society than in most others of a high degree of complexity. Secondly, the valuation and its expression in recognition and status, of ability and achievement by such universalistic standards as technical competence has, particularly in the occupational field, a far wider scope in modern Western society than in most others. No other large-scale society has come so near universalizing 'equality of opportunity'. An important consequence of the universalistic pattern in these two fields is the very high degree of social mobility, of potentiality for each individual to 'find his own level' on the basis of his own abilities and achievements, or, within certain limits, of his own personal wishes rather than a compulsory traditional status.

(Parsons, 1964, p. 82)

It is clearly just as easy to get carried away by the idea of selection as it is by the idea of discrimination. Just as partisan opponents of discrimination can find the thing they dislike throughout the labour market, so those sociologists who see selection as a good thing tend to see it as characteristic of the way labour markets work (see also Sowell, 1981a, 1981b).

Another example is provided by the work of an English writer on racial and ethnic relations, Michael Banton. Banton neatly exposes the faults of arguments which would have us see discrimination everywhere (Banton, 1983a, pp. 366–89; Banton 1983b). He points out, for instance, that such arguments neglect to make a distinction between 'categorical discrimination' in which employers use people values as the basis of their recruitment decisions and 'statistical discrimination' in which they do not. Statistical discrimination occurs as a by-product of the employers' use of work values. Employers want to select the best people for the job but find it costly to get hold of the information about job-seekers that they need. They therefore take a short-cut and use the category membership of job applicants in place of first-class information. Employers think that they know most members of a particular racial or ethnic category are more or less suitable for the job. This is not, in itself, (any sort of) discrimination, however.

Statistical discrimination only occurs in those cases where employers *mistakenly* exclude those (few or many) members of the category which they see as unsuitable who actually are suitable for the job in question (Banton, 1983a, pp. 369–70). For example, a number of highly qualified black workers in the United Kingdom and the United States will be excluded from jobs which they are quite capable of doing because most black workers in these countries are not as suitable for these jobs as whites. Employers are simply not willing to bear the costs of using a less clumsy device than 'race' to help them in selection.

Now Banton may well be correct to conclude that statistical discrimination is 'possibly the most important of the influences on the demand side' (1983a, p. 387). In any event, selection is an important labour market process. The problem which many sociologists have identified in Banton's analysis lies in the way he describes the actions of employers which produce statistical discrimination: he says these actions are 'rational'. That is (like Parsons, quoted above), Banton applies the language of positive evaluation to a labour market process in much the same way as anti-racists apply a negative evaluation to a labour market process. Indeed, Banton goes on to elaborate a theory which seeks to explain all of the labour market actions of employers and job-seekers in terms of 'rational choice' (cf. Heath, 1976). While Banton might argue (Banton, 1985) that the positive evaluation of rational actions is made by his readers, and is no part of his explanation, it is hard to believe that he could not take steps in advance to make certain that misinterpretation was impossible because he was unaware of the dangers of such mistakes. Such care is, however, characteristic of the final explanation of labour market workings we will consider.

Matching

If we believe that the fundamental nature of labour markets can be understood in terms of market values, then we will explain the workings of labour markets in terms of these values. In the

Weberian view, labour markets work through those signs of market positions which have legitimacy for everyone but aren't even proxies of merit in reality. Labour market patterns represent attempts to operate these legitimate criteria. This operation is best described as 'matching'. The term has been borrowed from Granovetter (1981; also see other chapters in Berg, 1981) because it seems to describe most accurately how sociologists think labour markets work when they are based on market values: what happens is not discrimination, or selection, but rather the market matches workers to jobs and vice versa.

·In the emphasis on the necessary legitimacy of labour market processes, it is clear that Weberian sociologists are usually anxious to avoid any hint of evaluation. They simply wish to show that it is how society evaluates these processes that matters and whether sociologists think them good or bad is neither here nor there. As a result, writing in this vein tends to avoid value-judgements of any kind; these sociologists are much less likely to use pejorative terms or positive ones (like 'merit') in their analysis of labour market processes (cf. Parkin, 1979, for example pp. 70–1). This does not, however, mean that Weberian sociologists are necessarily better equipped to avoid the mistake of explaining everything that happens in labour markets in terms of their pet theory.

Certain writers (for example Giddens, 1981; for general criticism of Giddens, and Parkin, see Stewart *et al.*, 1985) seek to explain every aspect of labour market workings in terms of what we have here called 'matching'. For example, it is not discrimination that results in the peculiar labour market patterns associated with gender but evidence of differences in 'market capacity' associated with gender (Garnsey, 1982, p. 439). Similarly, the sort of 'skill' that matters in the labour market is always a labour market type of skill and it is this that explains the (curious) labour market patterns that are associated with differences in education and training for example. There is no place for selection.

CONCEPTUAL INFLATION

In this chapter we have discussed a considerable variety of sociological theories. We first considered theories which sought to explain the importance of social groups, relations and institutions in the labour market in terms of the key sociological concepts of power and culture. In the second place, we considered three alternative theories (people, work and markets) of the basis of value in social hierarchy. Finally, we looked at three theories of the workings of labour markets which arose from sociologists' views of the basis of social hierarchy: discrimination, selection and matching. It will now be demonstrated that, in any of these categories, a useful theory can be made completely useless by 'conceptual inflation', that is by making the idea which is central to the theory cover too much ground (see Miles, 1989, p. 41–68; Mills, 1959). This usually happens when theorists want to cope with contradictory evidence without reducing the potential scope for the application of the theory they favour.

Two examples of conceptual inflation should suffice to explain both what the term means and why it is so dangerous. All of the theories discussed above have been disabled by inflation at some time, but the theory I have chosen as the first example is the feminist theory of the importance of a particular sort of person value (gender) in the labour market discussed on pp. 60–1 above.

Critics of a people value argument like the feminist theory might begin by asking whether there is not also a process whereby jobs are used as a source of value (and hence of hierarchy) rather than people: for example, is it not the evaluation of the job that comes first, then the observation that men or women do it, and then the conclusion that men or women have a certain value as workers? But, if they turn to conceptual inflation in defence, the proponents of the type of theory we were discussing as an example of people values can reply that this only *seems* to be the case.

They will argue that this sort of thing is in reality a secondary phenomenon, an example of a limited sort of 'feedback' which could not happen at all if people were not being used as the source of value and hierarchy. Firstly, the secondary phenomenon is *caused* by the use of people as the source of value (Baron, 1975; Barron and Norris, 1976). People can use jobs to grade only when the basis of value is established and this basis consists, of course, in differences between people. Without this foundation it would be impossible to use jobs as a source of value. For example, people may look at a particular job and judge it to be of low value but they are only doing this because it was a female job in the first place.

Secondly, the secondary phenomenon only has *results* because people are the source of value. Thus the limited use of jobs to grade people never alters the basic grades assigned to jobs according to a people-based value like gender. It only 'works', that is, has any results at all, when it does not alter these grades; and the only results it can have consist in confirming the use of people to grade. Jobs are only a source of value when the hierarchy that might result merely repeats what has been determined anyway.

To put it another way, the use of jobs to grade can only operate as 'positive feedback': a job has low value therefore women (who do the job) are most definitely lower value workers. 'Negative feedback' which challenges the assumption that gender is the source of value never has an effect. For example, the observation that the prime minister of the United Kingdom was a woman produced no results. Margaret Thatcher was, rather, the exception that proved the rule (that gender matters): it was said that 'she was more like a man than a woman' and so on. Jobs are a source of value only when this use helps to reproduce the idea that people are the ultimate source of value.

Similarly (for all of the following see Bradley, 1989 and Dex, 1985), men may argue that women should be excluded from a job because of the requirements of the job, but inflated theory permits the reply that men are only arguing in this way because the job is under threat of a change of gender (cf. Cockburn, 1983). What is really at stake can be gleaned from the male incumbents' complaints about this being 'man's work' (and from arguments about the 'family wage' as far as paid employment in general is concerned – see Land, 1980). It may seem that men are using the job as a source of value but in reality they are simply trying to avert a circumstance (the influx of women) that may threaten the gender-identity of the job. If the majority of people doing it were women then there would be some danger that the gender of the job would change.

With conceptual inflation, the feminist theory of people values (or *any* other in fact) has become useless to us. First, the theory becomes useless because it is not testable. The foregoing example has shown that no evidence can disprove the feminist argument when it is inflated. A theory which we cannot disprove is circular, and therefore is no longer usable. Once this sort of error becomes general, the interpretation of evidence depends entirely on the theory we begin with. If we begin with a theory which says people are the source of value and then identify patterns of labour market experience we will find, for example, that men seem to get 'better' jobs than women. But if we were to look at these same patterns from the other side of the labour market – the 'labour market experience of employers' – we would also find other sorts of evidence: different jobs (patterns associated with type of work, pay and so on) are associated with types of worker – 'better' and 'worse' workers for example (higher paid jobs seem to get 'better' workers than lower-paid ones). This is also the case with patterns of employment and unemployment of course: workers with no qualifications or training are more likely be unemployed (for example, see OPCS, 1989b, pp. 187–8). It now becomes clear that 'better' is not so self-evident as we might once have thought, no matter whether we are talking about people or jobs.

Let us now consider a second example: the various theories of labour market workings, beginning with discrimination. We know that sociologists are not always careful to avoid judgements about workers, or more likely jobs ('better' jobs and 'worse' jobs) which quickly make their argument circular. For example, let us say we consider racism a very bad thing. We find racism in the labour market and so our theory is that people are the source of value. We therefore look for evidence of black people doing 'undesirable' jobs. Finding this 'evidence' may well involve us in making some judgements that other people do not necessarily share about a job: we may say it is undesirable (for example, ignore its good points) because this suits us and is what we expect to find. It is often investigators' own values that lead them towards conceptual inflation. If we begin with a dislike of racism we end up seeing all labour market workings as discrimination (see Banton, 1985 who rightly criticises Fevre on this point). Similarly, someone who thinks jobs are the source of value may make all sorts of unsupported assumptions about whether a worker is 'undesirable' or not.

If inflated theory is to be avoided, the idea of discrimination should only be used to describe labour market workings where it is clear that people values are being used (and it is selection where work values are being used; and matching where market values are being used). But the discussion of discrimination above (pp. 71–2) included a description of inflated theory where the concept of 'discrimination' was made to mean much more than this; where 'discrimination' was applied to every case of hiring and firing. Similar inflation was instanced in the discussion of Banton's analysis of selection and Giddens' and Garnsey's work on matching. In all of these cases, useful concepts are inflated to the point at which they cease to be useful. If these ideas are to be of some use to the sociology of labour markets we must make sure that discrimination, selection and matching apply only to the operation of people, work and market values respectively.

There is no way of choosing between circular theories and it is axiomatic that if a number of competing explanations all fit the evidence then none of them can be all of the explanation. But people do choose between such theories none the less. This sets us a different problem, but one to which we already know the solution. People choose between inflated theories on the basis of their own values. They forget, once more, what Weber wrote, earlier in this century, about the need for social scientists to avoid the intrusion of value judgements into analysis:

The constant confusion of the scientific discussion of facts and their evaluation is still one of the most widespread and also one of the most damaging traits of work in our field. The forgoing arguments are directed against this confusion, and not against the clear-cut introduction of one's own ideals into the discussion.

(Weber, 1949, p. 60)

CONCLUSIONS

As long as conceptual inflation is avoided, we are left with all the theories we have discussed in this chapter intact. This diversity is not a problem but a resource.[6] We began this chapter with two questions: how society makes labour markets happen (origin) and how society makes them what they are (nature). These two questions were answered in a variety of different ways but always together. In the terms of the example we used at the beginning of the chapter, territories turn out to be the origin as well as the nature of the labour market. They are the nature of the five labour market processes and their cause.

This all makes good sense. Labour demand and labour supply are never abstract (in the labour market at least), for example there is always a particular type of work to do (even 'labourer' is a particular type of work), so form can never be separated from origin in practice. This much is obvious after short reflection: we do not know of any labour market which does not have a nature (for example, does not have labour market territories). In more theoretical terms, this chapter has shown that work and workers are socially constructed and are different, and qualitatively different, precisely because they are socially constructed.

These ideas will be explored at greater length in subsequent chapters, here it only needs to be pointed out that the fact of labour markets' social construction explains why we need more than one sociological theory of labour markets. If we consider the value-base of labour markets, for example, we need different explanations of these value-bases (people, work and market) because different people construct the nature of the labour market in a variety of different ways at different times and in different places. For instance, Maurice *et al.* (1986) suggest that, in effect, people-values are used to choose workers in France (whereas job-values are used to get production – see Chapter 4), while in Germany the reverse happens: job-values are used to choose workers (and people-values are used to get production from the workers – see also Windolf and Wood, 1988).

In future chapters we will not be trying to establish whether one catch-all theory is right or wrong, but, rather, trying to find the key questions which we need to ask in order to give us the variety of theories we require. We will need many different theories to explain real labour markets, even to explain a single labour market: a variety of specific, concrete instances of labour markets means we need a variety of theories. Fortunately, it is possible to build up a portfolio of theories, and to have different or competing theories at our disposal is not a disaster but an absolute necessity. We must learn how to generate (rather than get rid of) this theoretical variety. We do this by finding out what makes theories differ. We have already several such bases of difference: for example the key role of different answers to the questions of 'what is the basis of value' and 'how is value enforced'? The different answers to these questions give us different theories and the three sets of theories will be able to do much to explain labour market variety. We must repeat this process in the chapters which follow: we must find the questions to ask in order to generate a diversity of theories.

NOTES

1. Both principles discussed here are also essential (pre-) conditions for the further developments of labour markets discussed in later chapters, For example, without the social division of labour there would be no exchange, and no occupations, and no industries or firms. Without social hierarchy there would be no jobs as we know them.
2. In this chapter we are primarily concerned with labour and not just paid employment. Our discussion will turn to jobs (in Chapter 4) when we have discussed another form of division of labour which I will call 'economic'.
3. Just as in the case of the social division of labour, social hierarchy has always been of profound interest to sociologists, and, as before, each theory of social hierarchy is usually identified with a 'grand theory' (also see pp. 75–9 below). In this case the problem is usually discussed as one of social stratification and any consideration of labour markets is only a by-product. Detailed discussion of stratification is, of course, not the aim of this book.
4. For a sober assessment of the extent of, and trends in, gendered work in the United Kingdom see Crompton and Sanderson (1990).
5. A similar distinction could be made in respect of what might be called 'left-Weberian' thinking which is concerned to emphasise that, while people may well think that markets are better or fairer, the important point to grasp is that markets are definitely *not* better or fairer. Thus Berg (1971) and Jewson and Mason (1986) strike notes of moral outrage when they discuss the way in which the working class, for example, suffer from the dominance of rational, legal and universal criteria in the labour market.
6. Readers are referred to the Appendix – 'Societal Analysis as a Tool' – of Maurice *et al.* (1986) for a broader exposition of similar themes to those discussed below.

4

WORKERS AND JOBS

The previous chapter made little reference to *exchange*, the process whereby goods and services which we did not produce become our own when we pay for them in money or in kind (for a much more sophisticated discussion of exchange see, for example, Hodgson, 1988, pp. 148–9 *et seq.*). Nevertheless, the development of exchange was assumed in much of the discussion in the preceding chapter since without it there can be no buying and selling. Without exchange production only occurs for use, but once exchange develops then goods can become *commodities* which are produced for exchange rather than for use. This commodity exchange creates the broad basis of modern industries and occupations (cf. Marx 1976, pp. 470–80): the exchange of corn for handicraft goods, for example, provides the basis of the division between agriculture and industry. All of this is (indirectly) necessary for labour markets, but what is of most interest in this chapter is the exchange of one particular, and peculiar, commodity – labour.

In simple terms there would be no labour markets were it not for the exchange of labour. This exchange leads to the development of a new (economic) aspect of the division of labour: the division of labour between jobs (places for which labour is bought and sold) and between workers (categories of labour which are bought and sold). This *economic* division of labour only comes into being together with exchange because it requires that many things, but especially labour, be bought and sold. Whereas the social division of labour simply requires that not everyone produces the same things, in the economic division of labour people must produce different things *for sale*. People are divided into those who produce one good for sale and not another, *and* into those who must sell their labour and those who buy labour.

SOCIAL GROUPS, RELATIONS AND INSTITUTIONS

The introduction to this chapter would excite little debate between sociologists, but, just as in Chapter 3, consensus is under threat once we turn to analysis of social groups, relations and institutions. Any theory will seek to explain the same interdependent phenomena: the creation of a group of people who want to sell their labour and of a group of people who want to buy labour (both groups are necessary for exchange). But what one sees as important in the development of the exchange of labour dictates the way one sees the economic division of labour, and ultimately one's explanation of the workings of the labour market.

This connection arises because the development of exchange, and of the exchange of labour in particular, gives rise to the development of new social groups (of employers, of workers, firms, occupational groups, trade unions and so on), to new social relations (for example, between capital and labour), and to new social institutions (such as employment, or systems of training or industrial relations). These groups, relations and institutions would not arise without exchange and the economic division of labour, but different sociologists have, for example, attended to different groups and so have therefore drawn our attention to the role of these different groups in the workings of labour markets.

This is all to the good: a variety of sociological explanations is not simply acceptable, but also vitally necessary (see pp. 79–81 above). For example, in the following pages we will investigate the possibility that differences between industries account for labour market variation: different sorts of industries want or need different things of the labour market, and they have different uses and criteria for the five labour market processes because they want or take different things from them. There is certainly a great deal of material which seems to suggest that labour markets do vary by industry in all sorts of ways (see, for example, Ashton *et al.*, 1990; Berg, 1981; Brown, 1984; Dex, 1985, 1987; Maurice *et al.*,

1986): there are differences in wages, in recruitment and training practices, in the proportions of temporary workers, and part-time workers, for example. 'Race', gender, and age of workers have all been observed to vary with the type of industry concerned, for instance with whether the industry is classified as a manufacturing industry or as part of the service sector. But none of this necessarily means that the cause of labour market variation always lies in differences between industries such as variations in type of product or technology. It may be that there are different sorts of firms in different industries and that it is the differences between firms that account for differences in the relationship of various industries to labour markets.

To summarise, whatever theory we consider, there will be a connection between one's view of the development of the exchange of labour and one's view of the nature of the labour market, because any explanation of the former will draw our attention towards the creation of particular social groups, relations and institutions which will then play a major part in our understanding of what labour markets are about. There is, however, an ever-present danger of conceptual inflation (see pp. 75–9 above) and its end-product, a forced choice between two (or more) 'grand theories'. It will become clear below that, at the most general level, we can become preoccupied with the division *between* buyers and sellers or *within* groups of buyers or sellers. In fact social groups and relations are not limited to the creation of two 'sides' of the labour market and buyers and sellers do not always constitute social groups (with relations one to another) at all. But nor are the producers of the same commodity, for example all those involved in a particular industry or enterprise, always part of the same social group.

As in the previous chapter, consensus disappears when theories are inflated and the proponents of different explanations begin to argue for the exclusive and universal application of their favoured theory. Readers will now realise that this error can easily be compounded. For example, an inflated idea from the previous chapter can be combined with one from this chapter to produce a synthetic 'grand theory' explanation, a variation of Marxist-feminism for example (cf. Hartman, 1979), which is believed to explain everything that requires explanation in the sociology of labour markets.

Readers might also like to note that there is no (internal) theoretical reason which necessarily leads to particular combinations of 'grand theory' like Marxist-feminism. For example, sociologists like Elster (1985) and Hechter (1983) have considered combinations of varieties of Marxism with rational choice theory (see p. 74 above) rather than combinations with theory such as feminism, which emphasises the importance of discrimination; and there is no theoretical reason why conceptual inflation should not lead, for instance, to a creed of 'new right feminism'. Such a compound of grand theory might conclude that labour market processes lead to 'employers having all the lousy workers (men) in the jobs where they need the best ones' whereas leftward-leaning feminists simply conclude that 'women have got all the lousy jobs'.

In the following pages we will discuss sociological explanations of labour markets in terms of the various social groups, relations and institutions which are created with the economic division of labour. We will do this under three headings: explanations which refer to *specialisation and cooperation* in the economic division of labour; explanations which refer to *exploitation and conflict* in the economic division of labour; and explanations which see the economic division of labour in terms of *legitimacy and the market*. If we were thinking of these different types of explanations as the product of competing 'grand theories', we would probably have used the headings 'Durkheimian', 'Marxist' and 'Weberian' (theory) instead; but this is exactly the sort of approach we must avoid if we are to arm ourselves against conceptual inflation. We do not want to see the various sociological explanations which are on offer as *competing* theories, but as equally valid theories in the abstract which can only become *alternatives* when we are considering the evidence, that is, concrete evidence from a real labour market.

Specialisation and cooperation

It is possible to see commodity exchange as the consequence of the continued development of the specialisation which was discussed in Chapter 3 as an explanation of the origin of the social division of labour and of social hierarchy. If people, or groups of people, are specialising in particular aspects of the division of labour, they will consume a very limited range of goods if exchange does not develop. Exchange allows people to continue consuming a variety of things, even an increasing variety, while specialisation continues. Exchange is therefore a condition of further specialisation and the two become synonymous for all practical purposes.

In this view (see, for example, Smelser, 1963; and Offe, 1985; Rueschemeyer, 1986) the sociological explanation of the economic division of labour, in particular the explanation as to why people should begin to sell their labour, must refer to both force and something akin to choice. While dispossession from the 'means of production' (see p. 89 below) forces people to sell their labour, people may also choose to stop producing things (for use or for sale) because they can see that it is more efficient for others to specialise in the organisation of production while they sell their labour. Labour therefore becomes a commodity as part of the natural further development of specialisation. Families may begin by specialising in the production of particular commodities which they exchange, but some family members soon find it more rewarding to labour for wages. In time, some families do not actually produce commodities at all but produce labour instead, and gradually the family loses its production function altogether. The family loses its production function to new social groups called firms and the family is left with the function of producing labour (and also of consuming commodities). In order to emphasise the differentiation of function between social groups, this process is sometimes called 'structural differentiation' (Smelser, 1959, 1963).[1]

Where this point of view can be shown to be valid, the relationship between those who are made wage-labourers by structural differentiation and those who pay their wages is often not seen as a problem. There is nothing to be said about exploitation or unequal conflict because the relevant social relationships do not exist between two 'sides' but within a social group. The alternative name for that group, *company* rather than firm, suggests where sociological explanation lies: a firm is a company of people engaged in a common enterprise of production who share the same interests and whose relationships are distinguished by cooperation rather than conflict.

A new social group (the firm or company) is created in the economic division of labour. The company is an aggregate of people, each fulfilling their 'qualitatively different role specialisations' (see pp. 62–4 above), who are cooperating together to fulfil a joint function in the economic division of labour. If the economic division of labour is understood in these terms, then labour markets are understood to reflect the requirements of specialisation and cooperation.

For example, much variation and change can be explained simply in terms of the progress towards a more complex economic division of labour, for instance, by typing certain aspects of labour demand or supply as 'traditional' or 'modern'. Thus the distinction between 'traditional' and 'modern' industries might be used to explain the significance (for labour markets) of age differences between industries. In such examples it is argued that (whatever the unit, industry or firm/company) modernity is represented by a cooperative relationship between people filling qualitatively different role specialisations, and variations, and change, are to be explained in terms of approximation to, or departure from, this ideal: for example country A is better at it than country B, industry A better than industry B, firm A better than firm B, and so on. But this is not the only type of explanation of change and variation which is open to sociologists who refer to specialisation and cooperation in the economic division of labour.

The transition from old to new forms is not without difficulty and these transitional problems can provide the basis of sociological explanations. For example, once the family ceases to be the unit of production the question immediately arises of *who* will allocate labour? If the family no longer performs these functions, allocating labour by way of compulsion and obligation, then labour must be allocated in some other way. Ideally labour should be allocated by employers (see below), but the transition from the authority (in the allocation of labour) of the family to the authority of the firm, can be difficult and slow (Smelser, 1959). Indeed some writers have wondered whether allocation of labour by way of compulsion and obligation has survived so long that it cannot be seen as a transitional at all (see Corrigan, 1977; Miles, 1987).

Finally, structural-functionalist theory has often been explained in terms of an analogy which compares society to an organism.

For example, the company is not the only social group created by further specialisation: there are occupational groups too. These are collections of people who share the same place in the division of labour and who derive their identity from their voluntary association with others who fill the same role. In his discussion of the changing division of labour, Durkheim (1933) saw these occupational groups as a necessary part of the organism since they are required to keep it healthy.

Similarly, the firm or company can be seen as an organism to which all of its members make a necessary contribution. Although there may be no (real reason for) conflict in societies with an advanced (economic) division of labour, organisms can become sick (they can suffer the sickness of *anomie* for example) and pathological social forms are possible. Structural-functionalist theory therefore offers the possibility of explanations of the 'economy effects' on labour markets in terms of pathological deviation from the norm, and not simply in terms of the difference between traditional and modern forms or even the difficulties of transition from one to the other.

The most obvious example of an explanation of variation and change in labour supply in terms of sickness in the organism once more concerns the allocation of labour. Parsons (after Weber) remarks on the 'dangers' of the allocation and direction of labour being taken over by employees rather than managers when the family loses this function along with the function of production (Parsons, 1964, pp. 46–8; for contemporary evidence of employees' role in recruitment in some European countries see Maurice *et al.*, 1986; Windolf and Wood, 1988).

If workers profess to 'own' jobs, says Parsons, a pathological form has arisen and inefficiency will result. The proper agency for the efficient allocation and direction of labour is the locus of authority in the firm, the manager or employer. Nobody can enjoy the full benefits of specialisation if managers are not allowed to allocate labour. But there are problems here: the extent to which specialisation and cooperation are reflected in labour market processes can easily be exaggerated, as can the degree of specialisation and cooperation which are, in any case, involved in work in established industrial societies (cf. Braverman, 1974). Furthermore, the firm may be a social group but so are (informal) workers' organisations and (formal) trade unions. These are more than occupational groups, more (even) than pathological occupational groups. Whatever structural-functionalist theory says, there are social relations between people who sometimes conceive of themselves as being on different 'sides', in other words, as being in conflict rather than cooperating with one another. This much has even been admitted, albeit reluctantly, in those Eastern European countries which have recently undergone social, economic and political transformation (Neumann, 1989).

Exploitation and conflict

If the economic division of labour is to be understood in terms of exploitation and conflict, we begin by pointing out that the creation of a relationship between people who want to sell labour and people who want to buy labour occurs with the development of capitalist relations of production (Marx, 1976). Sellers, buyers, and the relationship between them, are created by the same process: the concentration of ownership of the 'means of production' in the hands of a few and the 'dispossession' or 'expropriation' of others. These others, the proletarians, lose their ownership of the means of production and have nothing to sell (no other commodity to sell) but their labour. Thus, in Chapter 1, Gabriel Oak sought work at the hiring fair because he lost his own farm and so was forced to sell, or try to sell, his labour for wages. The bourgeoisie, on the other hand, own the means of production but must buy the labour of others if they are to accumulate capital. There is mutual dependency here, but there is also (hidden) exploitation and (potential for) conflict.

Sellers and buyers certainly need each other but where does the exploitation arise? According to Marxist theory exploitation arises in the way that the bourgeoisie accumulate capital: they can only do this by paying proletarians less than the value of their labour. This is described as exploitation and the existence of this exploitation means that conflict is built into the system. As long as capital is accumulated through exploitation, it is in the interests of each side to fight over the degree of exploitation (for example over pay, or over how hard people are supposed to work) and indeed to fight over the right (in principle) of those who buy labour to exploit those who sell it.

In this conflict, the two sides (bourgeoisie and proletariat, or capital and labour) are unequally matched. The relationship between workers and employers is one of mutual interdependence, exploitation *and* inequality in terms of economic power (also see Offe, 1985 who considers this inequality the *sine qua non* of labour markets). The employer has much more real freedom to choose between workers than the employees have to choose between employers. Furthermore, unlike the employers (who can choose to do something else for a living if the worst happens) the workers have no choice whether to take part in exchange or not: if they do not work then they will starve.

In practice though, capitalists do not often wish to see proletarian families starve. Since they need a continual supply of labour, capitalists need proletarians to come to work, more-or-less fit for labour, day after day and generation after generation: in capitalism 'labour power' must be reproduced (for a general discussion of reproduction see Purdy, 1988). Obviously, capitalists want this reproduction to be done cheaply since the less expensive the reproduction of labour power is, the smaller the (share of) wages which need to be paid to make this reproduction possible. There are, however, some types of labour that can be reproduced (at least in part) without the help of wages paid by capitalists. This is the case, for example, where peasant families occasionally provide wage-labourers but subsist, for the most part, outside the capitalist system. These workers are a part of the 'reserve army of labour' (Marx, 1976, pp. 794–802) and they can clearly be exploited at a higher rate as long as they are not fully incorporated into the 'active army of labour' (at which point there is no longer a subsidy to the costs of reproducing labour power). Something similar might be said of those members of the reserve army of labour whose subsistence, when unemployed, is paid for by the state; but in this case capitalists will contribute to the costs of subsistence in one way or another.

Theories which concern themselves with the reproduction of labour power, are, in effect, concerned with what happens 'before' the labour market; but explanations of labour markets in terms of exploitation and conflict may also be concerned with what happens 'after' the labour market, that is, with what happens inside the factory, shop or office. Instead of understanding the division of labour inside a firm or organisation as reflecting 'qualitatively different role specialisations', this type of theory sees this aspect of the division of labour, variously called the 'manufacturing', 'technical' or 'detail' division of labour (see Marx, 1976, pp. 475–7), as a location for exploitation and conflict. Certainly, workers who undertake different tasks must cooperate, but there is assumed to be continued pressure from capitalists to increase the division of labour in the individual firm in order to increase exploitation. This tendency therefore gives further cause for conflict.

In the 'detail' division of labour an individual worker (or an individual machine) does not produce a commodity; workers (or machines) only produce commodities through their cooperative efforts, each making a part, or detail of the commodity. For Marx, and other political economists, increase in the detail division of labour was more-or-less a law of capitalist development. Capitalist competition ensured that the increased division of labour within the factory, together with the progressive application of technology to work, would increase productivity and guarantee the evermore efficient use of resources. But Marx was, of course, concerned to emphasise the exploitation which he saw as inherent in 'capitalist relations of production'. In his view (Marx, 1976, pp. 293–306) capitalist production entailed two processes: the labour process, in which 'use-values' were created, and the process of creating value.[2] In simple terms, the process of creating value makes money whereas the labour process makes things, but in capitalism you cannot have one without the other. In this schema, the detail division of labour allows capitalists to make more things and to extract more 'surplus value'.

At least three varieties of explanations of labour markets arise from the general approach described above. Firstly, there are explanations which seek to increase our understanding of labour markets by categorising them as capitalist or not, or as more capitalist and less capitalist. For example, labour markets may vary according to whether the employers who use them are large capitalists (perhaps even monopoly capitalists) or the self-employed, bosses of partnerships or family firms, or the owners of franchises. Similarly, labour markets may be different where firms are communally owned (as in cooperatives) or owned by the state (also see Chapter 5 below). Similar explanations can also be developed to demonstrate the importance of differences in the degree of incorporation of workers into the capitalist system, especially the degree to which their labour is reproduced in that system, on the supply side of the labour market. The case of peasant-workers was mentioned above, but we might also think of other groups of workers like migrants, and perhaps women (Beechey, 1978, 1987), who may not be fully incorporated into a capitalist system of production.

Secondly, there are explanations of labour markets in terms of the things done by capitalists to exploit workers, especially, to raise the level of exploitation. Thus there are labour market theories that refer to employers' recruitment strategies which are designed to get hold of the most 'exploitable' workers or the workers who can be entrusted with the job of exploiting others on capital's behalf. Similarly, some explanations refer to the way in which work and technology in the individual firm or organisation is designed in order to increase exploitation. This is assumed to have profound effects on labour markets, for example to decrease the demand for particular categories of labour or even for labour as a whole.

Finally, there are a number of explanations which seek to analyse labour markets in terms of the unequal conflict between capital and labour (see, for example, Garnsey *et al.*, 1985). This conflict can extend to the labour market (much conflict in the labour market is theorised as part of a broader conflict over work and technology) or may even begin there. Thus some work on employers' strategies assumes that there is conflict over control in the workplace, and that, although bosses are generally in command, they have to fight for their control, for instance by using 'divide and rule' tactics which, once more, have clear labour market effects. Other theories return to the supply side and point out that different groups of workers have different relationships with their employers: some are not as conflict-ridden as others.

In sum, theories which explain the workings of labour markets in terms of the conflict between capital and labour explain variation and change by pointing to variation in the extent of conflict and/or to differences in strategies evolved to deal with conflict. In this way, theories of conflict between capital and labour can help to explain variation and change by industry, and even by occupation or firm or subgroup of workers. But there are problems with this type of theory, at least in a pure form. The more it is applied to real cases, the more the initial assumptions (about exploitation and conflict) of the theory must be qualified. For example, some sociologists have gone on to investigate the strategies used by employers in the labour market which are intended to ensure the *cooperation* of workers. It is a matter of debate whether such work belongs in this subsection or in the previous discussion of specialisation and cooperation.

Legitimacy and the market

Finally, we turn to those theories which appear to analyse the workings of labour markets in terms of similar causes for both 'sides' (capital and labour) while still recognising the existence of the two 'sides'. As before, the labour market sociology flows from a theory of the economic division of labour.

In Weberian theory (Weber, 1964, 1968), the rise of commodity exchange necessarily entails the acceptance of rational, legal and universal criteria as legitimate bases of social action. In the present context, much the most important of these criteria is the market itself (any market, not simply the labour market). Without the acceptance of markets as legitimate mechanisms by which resources can be distributed, goods cannot be bought or sold and there is no exchange.

The exchange of labour, and hence the creation of a market for labour, is a special case of the general rule. It requires that the market be accepted as a legitimate mechanism for determining the allocation of labour. Indeed, Marx remarked, perhaps a little hastily, that 'modern society has no other rule, no other authority for the distribution of labour than free competition' (from *The Poverty of Philosophy*, quoted by Rattansi, 1982, p. 18). Furthermore, since labour is no ordinary commodity, it also requires that people should come to accept as legitimate the notion that their labour be bought and sold. In other words, it is important that the idea of two 'sides' of the labour market should be seen as acceptable – put very simply, people must *want* to buy and sell labour.

In fact, we oversimplify the Weberian view if we refer to people 'wanting to sell labour'. This implies something close to the free choice to labour which we discussed above and the Weberian view lies somewhere between such a choice and the compulsion assumed in the Marxist analysis. For example, Weberians might agree with structural-functionalists who argue that specialisation frees people to work outside the family, but would be far less inclined to assume that people will sell their labour just because they can sell their labour.

Similarly, Weberian theory agrees with the observation of political economists like Marx that some people are deprived – by what Weber calls 'social closure' (cf. pp. 57–8 above) – of the chance to become capitalists and so there are people who are not in the category of buyers of labour even if they are not yet sellers. That they are not yet sellers follows from Weber's opinion that dispossession is neither sufficient nor necessary to the creation of free wage labour.

Historical evidence suggests that many people have been prepared to sell their labour when they still had alternative ways of earning a living like commodity production on their own account. Furthermore, history tells of people who continued to produce goods for subsistence or exchange when it was increasingly obvious to others that this would lead to ruin and starvation (see, for example, Bythell, 1969, 1978). It seems that such cases are only the extreme examples of a sort of cultural resistance to free wage labour (see, for example, Thompson, 1967, 1974) and all that is entailed in selling labour, and it was this resistance that had to be overcome. In other words, people had to be persuaded that it was legitimate for them to sell labour (as well as, or instead of, being forced to do it or simply seeing that it was preferable). But if there are people prepared to sell labour, labour markets also require people who will buy that labour.

Weber's account of the *Protestant Ethic and the Spirit of Capitalism* (1930) is well known. His thesis is that cultural resistance to the buying and selling of labour can be as strong amongst those who might buy labour as it is amongst those who sell it: it will not be seen as legitimate without the acceptance of rational, legal and universal criteria (including the acceptance of the legitimacy of the market mechanism) as a guide to social action. Only then can a prospective employer accept what to us might seem the self-evident good sense of buying the labour of others in order to produce commodities for sale and for profit. Only then, moreover, will the labour market be accepted as a legitimate way of finding labour (legitimate, for example, because it is deemed efficient and therefore satisfies a rational aim).

Weberian theory is not directly concerned with questions of exploitation and conflict within the labour market, once established. Instead, the question is the same as before: just as we asked how buying and selling labour came to be seen as legitimate, so we now ask how is the legitimacy of the workings of labour markets achieved and maintained? The answer is also the same as before: the question of exploitation and unequal conflict does not arise since the market helps to legitimate the relations between both 'sides' because it satisfies rational, legal and universal criteria – both in principle (the idea of a market) and in practice (the way in which labour markets work on a day-to-day basis). In simple terms, if inequality is perceived in the economic division of labour then it is only inequality of outcomes, and the process which produces inequality can still be regarded as 'fair' and 'efficient' (and so satisfy any rational, legal and universal criteria against which such outcomes might be judged).

Readers will see that in Weberian theory the legitimacy of labour markets is explained in a consistent way: both sides accept labour markets as legitimate for the same reasons (for example because of their 'fairness' and their 'efficiency'). The changes in social organisation which accompany the creation of labour markets are theorised in much the same way, no matter whether we are talking about social organisation with reference to labour demand or labour supply.

According to this view, labour markets reflect the fact that people have to see them as *legitimate* mechanisms. Furthermore, the rational, legal and universal form of authority, the authority which gives the modern labour market its legitimacy, explains much that is characteristic of labour markets, for example the forms of competition into which job-seekers enter.

Finally, progress from other forms of authority to rational, legal and universal forms helps to explain labour market change and variation. For example, it explains the increased use of formal methods in the labour market (open advertising of vacancies using the press or the public employment service, formal application and interview procedures) and the decline (but also see Fevre, 1989a) of informal methods (word of mouth recruitment and recommendation, cold calling and so on).

INDUSTRIAL VALUES

In Chapter 3 we discussed the social principles which sociologists believe provide the basis of our understanding of the contribution of studies of *society* to the explanation of the origins and nature of labour markets. We then went on to discuss the *social values* which arise on the foundation of the social division of labour and social hierarchy: people values, work values and market values.

In the first half of the current chapter we have begun our investigation of the ways in which sociologists understand the contribution of economy to the origins and nature of labour markets in terms of specialisation and cooperation, exploitation and conflict, and legitimacy and the market. As in Chapter 3, we can now go on to consider the question of values, in this case *industrial* values. These are industrial rather than social values in that they do not arise simply on the basis of the two social principles (the social division of labour and social hierarchy) described in the previous chapter. Industrial values do not arise without the additional developments of exchange and the economic division of labour between workers and between jobs which has been described above. Because people become workers, on the one hand, and employers with jobs to fill on the other, they develop industrial values.

Unlike social values, industrial values do not provide a basis for hierarchies of people and hierarchies of different types of work. We can take an example to illustrate this point. In Chapter 3 we discussed work values, the particular category of social values which forms the basis of social hierarchies based on differences between types of work, for example the differences in usefulness, or differences in degree of difficulty, of work (factors which are often assumed to be correlated of course), which are sometimes used to grade work and people. In the current chapter we will shortly introduce a category of industrial values which we will call *technical values* which may immediately recall the work values of Chapter 3 but actually plays a completely different role in the construction of labour market processes.

Consider, for example, the part played by technical values in the decisions made by an employer who uses technical values to order priorities, that is, who decides whether one thing is better than another because of technical considerations such as the requirements of the technology the firm uses. The firm may use technology which requires highly skilled workers. Our employer considers this factor as the determining influence on his or her decisions and so develops an internal labour market (ILM) in order to train and retain the highly skilled workers he or she needs.

In this example technical values lead to an ILM, but these technical values tell us nothing about the social basis on which the employer will recruit workers at the point of entry to the ILM. He or she may do this on the basis of people values, work values or market values. Further discussion of this point can be found at the end of this chapter, but for the moment the simple conclusion readers should draw from the comparison between work and technical values is that industrial values as a whole do not provide the basis of hierarchies but that theories of social hierarchies are not intended to explain all that can be explained in the sociology of labour markets. We might know, for instance, that people values matter in a particular labour market, but we will also want to know why a particular number of workers find jobs on the basis of these values and why some of the jobs are permanent and some are simply casual. To answer these and other, related questions, we must attend to the industrial values of employers *and* workers.[3]

The three categories of industrial values considered below are *economic* values, *technical* values, and *organisational* values, however there are only two subsections and these deal with technical and organisational values respectively. The investigation of the effects of economic values is, of course, properly the province of economics and not of sociology. Rather a lot of this book has already been devoted to the work of economists, so there will be no subsection on economic values. Nevertheless, it is impossible to exclude the subject entirely and so the following pages will include some discussion of interdisciplinary work that refers to both technical and economic values or to organisational and economic values.

If it is impossible to entirely exclude economics from what follows, it is even more difficult to exclude economists. Certainly, the investigation of how industrial values affect, and are affected by, social groups, relations and institutions has been the stock-in-trade of much sociological research into the workings of labour markets; and work which refers to specialisation and cooperation, exploitation and conflict, and legitimacy and the market will be considered in each category of industrial values. Nevertheless, readers will quickly see that much of the path-finding research was actually done by economists, indeed economics as well as sociology is represented in the three recent pieces of research I have chosen to provide many of the illustrations in the following pages (Ashton *et al.*, 1990; Dex, 1987; Windolf and Wood, 1988).

Technical values

Both workers and employers know that the technical values of coal mining in twentieth-century America are different from those of coal mining in nineteenth-century America. New technology and changes in work organisation have altered the technical values in the industry: for example, work at the coal face is not as dangerous or as arduous as it once was. Similarly, one modern industry differs from another: there are differences in work organisation and technology between firms that produce computer software and those that are engaged in the continuous process production of chemicals. The proof that technical values affect labour markets is to be found in the different sorts of labour markets we find for jobs in computer software and jobs in the chemical industry (Kuhn, 1989; Nichols and Beynon, 1977).

When we speak of technical *values* in relation to labour market processes we refer only indirectly to the requirements of particular technologies and ways of organising work. For the most part, the theories discussed in this subsection are sociological theories of the way in which technical values affect the behaviour of social groups and the shape of social relations and institutions. Such theories cannot, therefore, be seen as technologically determinist, but this does not mean that they are above criticism.

Before we examine examples of research under this heading, one or two words of warning are necessary concerning the use of the idea of 'skill' in this research (for elaboration, see Rose, 1988). In the first place, work which assumes that the skill required of a job, or possessed by a worker, is self-evident and is simply a reflection of the technical requirements of particular kinds of labour has recently received much criticism.[4] In the second place, it often seems that technical values are all too frequently reduced to questions of (the presence or absence of) skill when in fact there are other technical values like working conditions, for instance aspects of health and safety, which are also used to inform the decisions of workers and employers. The consequences of this sort of neglect are potentially serious. When a sociologist argues that some work has been 'degraded' because the skill entailed in that work is less than it once was (see the discussion of Braverman below), he or she may produce a misleading impression if they leave us in ignorance of any changes in working conditions which have accompanied this 'degradation'. Certainly there is automation in coal mining and some skills are no longer used by coal miners, but if there is also a better record of health and safety (in what nevertheless remains a dangerous industry), should we conclude that work in this industry has been 'degraded'?

Bearing this warning in mind, we begin with those theories which suggest that type of technology and type of work organisation determines the quantity of labour demand. In Chapter 1, we encountered the idea that the amount of technology (a firm can be 'capital intensive' or 'labour intensive') or the level of technology (new or old, high or low) determines whether employers will use a lot of labour or a little. Modern industries are assumed to have more technology, to be more capital intensive, than traditional ones and so use less labour than traditional industries for a given volume of production. On the other hand, modern economies have growing service sectors, and service sector industries are much less capital intensive than manufacturing industries.

Various writers have also suggested that the type of technology and the type of work organisation also determine the quality of labour demanded. For example, Ashton *et al.* (1990) found that young workers were largely excluded from capital-intensive manufacturing plants which had twenty-four hour working, but were more popular in industries which had low skill requirements.

Following Braverman (1974), it has often been suggested that modern technology requires *less* skill and that workers in capitalist societies are becoming 'deskilled' and their work is becoming 'degraded'. This view contrasts with that advanced in an earlier chapter of this book where levels of skill were assumed to vary directly with levels of technology. Thus in Chapter 2, we encountered some variations on a theory in labour market economics which suggests that, as far as labour markets are concerned, industries or firms (or even parts of firms) can be categorised according to the type of technology or work organisation used because technology and work organisation directly affect the use employers make of labour markets (see Gordon, 1972). For example, readers were reminded above of the idea that firms with lots of technology need to hold on to their skilled workers, and so make use of internal labour markets, whereas firms with little technology have few skilled workers and have no use for internal labour markets (or, perhaps, for any care in recruitment procedures at all).

This 'dualist' theory is clearly concerned with the determining effects of technical values: employers in the (high technology) 'primary' sector have different values to those in the 'secondary' sector. Indeed, employers in the secondary sector might not appear to have technical values to guide them at all. Something similar might be said of the two groups of workers identified in dualist explanations. In dual labour market theory it is often assumed, for example, that 'secondary workers' do not want skilled work or stable employment situations and prefer to move from one lowly job to another. They will make extensive use of external labour markets but have no interest in ILMs.

A variation on this theme can also be used to distinguish two groups of skilled workers: those with transferable skills which are of use to more than one employer, and those with non-transferable skills which are specific to one organisation. Workers with transferable skills are much more likely to make (successful) use of external labour markets (Harris *et al.*, 1987). Althauser and Kalleberg (1981) offer the related notion of *firm* ILMs which give workers access to many, although not all, of the jobs in a particular firm, and *occupational* ILMs which provide access to jobs in several firms (also see Ashton, 1986). Such theories do not necessarily imply that workers are exercising real choices between technical values. Indeed Norris (1978a, 1978b) notes that the presence or absence of skills of any kind need not be seen as an aspect of workers' 'personal characteristics' but rather as a result of previous labour market experience. For example, whether or not one becomes skilled (or, indeed, gains a transferable skill instead of a non-transferable one) may depend in large part on (local) labour market conditions at the time of one's first entry to the labour market.

Nevertheless, it is clear enough that technical values can be as important in explaining the behaviour of workers as they are in explanations of employers' behaviour. Workers frequently argue that change in recruitment patterns which is associated with changes in work organisation and/or technology will bring about the 'dilution of labour', a bad thing when judged according to certain technical values (an argument which is implicit in Braverman's thesis, of course). This was, after all, one of the arguments advanced by the Luddites who resisted change in technology and work organisation in the early years of the Industrial Revolution on the grounds that 'unapprenticed' women and youths would take over their work at a lower level of skill *and* would produce an inferior product (Thompson, 1974). In more recent times, managers (amongst others) have used their position in the production system to shelter them from unemployment: they are able to save themselves when redundancy threatens by arguing that there will still be something for them to do while other workers are more explicitly identified with particular tasks which are no longer deemed necessary (Schervish, 1983). In other words, managers are able to mobilise technical values in their defence.

It is now becoming obvious that theories which refer to the importance of technical values need not be dualist theories, and nor must they necessarily refer to differences in skill. Bresnen *et al.* (1985) have researched the labour market effects of the peculiar technical values in particular industries. In the construction industry production is organised on a project basis and not as a process (where the latter has been attempted, for example with the introduction of process technology, the experiment has failed). According to Bresnen *et al.*, it therefore makes sense for employers in the construction industry to use temporary and casual workers.

Different types of employment (part-time instead of full-time, temporary instead of permanent, casual or even illegal instead of regular employment) often require that the employers who must fill vacancies and the workers who must find jobs, vary their methods. This point is made by Bresnen *et al.* when they conclude that not only do technical values lead construction employers to use labour markets for the peculiar purpose of recruiting temporary and casual workers, but they also use labour markets in a different way to employers in some other industries. For example, the construction employers' need to recruit large numbers of temporary and casual workers at periodic intervals leads them (and construction workers) to rely extensively on *informal* methods (Bresnen *et al.*, 1985, p. 114).

Theories of the labour market effects of decisions based on technical values need not refer to differences in technology at all, but simply to differences in work organisation which give rise to particular technical values. For example, differences in work organisation can be shown to produce different sorts of labour demand and thus labour market effects vary between different industries and firms. In the United Kingdom the hotel and catering industry recruits large numbers of part-time and temporary workers because the nature of this business is intermittent and seasonal.

Recent research in the United Kingdom has suggested that employers in a variety of industries have latterly started to give the technical values which lead to the employment of part-time and temporary workers more attention as they move towards the creation of a 'flexible' workforce in which employment patterns more closely reflect the pattern of production (Ashton *et al.*, 1990; Fevre, 1991). Such employers may shift to new informing and screening procedures which are more suited to the flexible model, but any significant change is more likely to have resulted from the effects of structural change in the proportions of employment taken up by different industries rather than from change at the level of the individual enterprise.

Dex's (1987) explanation for the increased employment of women in the United Kingdom also refers to the growth of alternatives to full-time, permanent employment. The shift of employment from manufacturing to services has increased demand for women workers who are prepared to work part-time. In similar vein, Ashton *et al.* (1990) show that the increase in part-time employment in the United Kingdom in the 1980s has coincided with reduced employment opportunities for younger workers.

Finally, we turn to some examples of interdisciplinary work which seeks to explain labour markets in terms of technical and economic values. We discussed above the influence of type of technology and work organisation on the quantity and quality of labour demand. In both cases it is frequently suggested that these influences only matter because it is cheaper (for employers) this way. For example, Jordan (1982) thinks that employers automate because it is cheaper to invest in technology than to pay wages; some 'labour process' theorists think it is cheaper to deskill than pay the wages of skilled workers; and some dualist economists discussed in Chapter 2 think it is cheaper for some employers to pay the wages of skilled workers because this allows them to use more productive (and profitable) high technology.

Dex (1987) finds that service sector firms have limited potential for productivity gains because they have little technology and are labour intensive. She concludes that such firms turn to women workers, that is to cheaper labour, because they are labour intensive: a smaller wage bill is in fact the obvious way to cut costs when productivity gains are limited. We noted that Ashton *et al.* found that younger workers were more popular in industries which did not require skilled workers, but this was not simply a case of employers responding to technical values because Ashton *et al.* point out that since these were low-skill industries cost mattered more. Employers in these industries actually preferred younger workers because they were cheaper (Ashton *et al.*, 1990, pp. 99–100).

The notion that some employers, perhaps those in the 'secondary' category of dualist theory, are not interested in technical values is also addressed by Thurrow. Thurrow argues that employers in the primary sector want to minimise the costs of wages *and* training. If we assume that job-seekers wait in line for primary sector vacancies, with the order in the queue decided by level of qualifications, then those workers with the most qualifications are hired first because they can be trained at least cost. The job queue reflects the fact that workers are in a situation of 'job-competition' for vacancies in the primary sector whereas in the secondary sector there are no dominant technical values and no queues. There is simply 'wage-competition' and the cheapest worker gets the job (Thurrow, 1975).

Further development of these ideas in American labour market research has generally been concerned with the different economic values which arise in competitive and non-competitive industries and with the labour market effects of monopoly in product markets or other limitations on competition.[5] In similar fashion, Windolf and Wood (1988) conclude that the two main causes of differences in, and changes in, recruitment systems are differences in, and changes in, production systems and product markets. Garnsey *et al.* (1985) also emphasise the importance of product markets as part of their general argument that workers and employers structure the labour market in a way that provides a hedge against risk and uncertainty (also see the discussion of Stark's work on pp. 127–8 below). Furthermore, the account of the explanation offered by Ashton *et al.* (1990) for the concentration of younger workers in particular industries is not yet complete. Ashton *et al.* think that there are few young workers in oligopolistic industries (where competition is limited), and more of these workers in competitive industries because it is here that cost (that is, economic values) matters. The largest numbers of younger workers are found where industries are competitive as well as requiring less skilled workers.

Finally, Bresnen *et al.* (1985) found that construction firms which required large numbers of temporary workers made use of informal methods of recruitment, but many researchers, including Windolf and Wood (1988) have pointed out that informal methods offer a cheap alternative to certain employers. The suggestion that cost is important in employers' choice of methods is also made by researchers who have looked at the way employers get rid of workers. For example, the low cost of getting rid of women and youths (they generally have shorter service and so qualify for less severance pay, they are also more likely to leave voluntarily) has been advanced as an explanation of why they are fired first, and even of why employers have hired them in the first place (just in case they need to sack workers cheaply). For example, Dex (1987) points out that having women who will leave at low cost is an easy way for manufacturing industry to shed labour.

Organisational values

The organisations which play a part in modern labour markets differ one from another. The organisations we call firms have a variety of different organisational forms: traditional family firms are not the same as modern bureaucratic ones and large firms have different organisations to small ones, for example – thus large firms are perhaps more likely to have ILMs (Cornfield, 1981; Wallace and Kalleberg, 1981). Similarly with trade unions: the organisation of a large, modern general trade union is not the same as that of a small, craft trade union (for a sophisticated example of analysis of differences in organisational values between unions see Offe, 1985). But, as in the previous subsection, the sociology of labour markets is not so much concerned with the direct effects of organisational differences but with the organisational *values* that arise on the basis of these differences (see Cornfield, 1987). For example, a family firm may not have all the different (hierarchical) levels of authority of a large public company, but what interests us most is not the missing levels but the form that authority takes in the family firm as opposed to the public company. In a family firm with a paternalist authority structure, people are meant to feel they are part of a family, whereas in a firm with a bureaucratic authority structure people are meant to follow bureaucratic rules (also see Bradley, 1990; Martin and Fryer, 1973; Rainnie, 1989). Thus Norris reminds us that paternalism cannot be maintained if employers are not seen to reward 'loyalty and good service' when recruiting to lower management positions (Norris, 1978c, p. 484). More to the point, Salais *et al.* (1986) tell how employers (and others) in France tried to transplant the organisational values of the farm, household and workshop to large enterprises.

It is clear that differences in organisational values have a great deal to do with labour markets. For instance, Cornfield (1981) notes the differences in lay-off procedures which are associated with different authority structures, and Windolf and Wood (1988) show the importance for recruitment practices of variations in organisational values between firms and changes in organisational values in particular industries, as in the increased use of bureaucratic values which has accompanied the concentration of business in the retail industry in the hands of a small number of large companies (for the United States see Bluestone and Stevenson, 1981). Ashton *et al.* (1990) make similar points and show how the replacement of family firms by large corporations in the UK retail industry (and also in hotels and catering) has led to a change in recruitment practices which has, in turn, resulted in the replacement of school-leavers by married women.

Such examples confirm that there is an association between organisational values and labour markets, but exactly how are these values believed to affect labour markets? The two most common answers to this question refer, respectively, to the notion of *strategy* and the notion of *custom*. Both ideas apply in equal measure in explanations of the way in which technical (and economic) values affect labour markets, of course; although this is mentioned less frequently in the literature.

The idea of strategy is not limited to the sociology of labour markets (see, for example, Crow, 1989), let alone to the investigation of the importance of organisational values to labour markets, but in this connection we refer simply to strategies designed by employers or workers to achieve goals set by organisational values. For example, managers may devise strategies which involve particular kinds of recruitment practices which are intended to maximise *control* over the workforce (see Hyman, 1987 and further discussion below).

By way of contrast, much writing on labour markets does not refer to the conscious, intentional planning activities implied by the idea of strategy, but to the unintentional, unconscious acceptance of tradition, of custom and practice for example. In the work of Windolf and Wood (1988) and that of Ashton *et al.* (1990) recruitment procedures are seen as customary practices. In this case organisational values are enshrined in the custom but they influence the behaviour of employers none the less.

Furthermore, customs – like strategies – can vary from firm to firm, industry to industry, and country to country (Cornfield, 1981; Windolf and Wood, 1988). For example, Maurice *et al.* note that personnel departments are less important in Germany than in France (where personnel staff undertake the initial hiring procedure; Maurice *et al.*, 1986, p. 141). Despite the observations of Salais *et al.* Maurice *et al.* conclude that the important observation to be made about French practices is that they are bureaucratic and centralised. In theory this should offer opportunities for social mobility but in practice bureaucracy (in France) produces job competition and limited mobility (Maurice *et al.*, 1986, p. 165).

Although much of the discussion below is (unfortunately) overreliant on the notion of strategy (see Hyman, 1987; cf. Offe, 1985), ideas of strategy and custom are not mutually exclusive (Garnsey *et al.*, 1985). For example, in common with many of their contemporaries, Ashton *et al.* (1990) have noted the attempts made by employers in the United Kingdom to change the 'culture' of their firms to make it more closely resemble the 'culture' of American or, more likely, Japanese firms. These employers say that they want their employees to identify more closely with their firms. Thus, when they recruit new workers, employers will look for evidence of this identification rather than, for example, for evidence of specific skills (Ashton *et al.*, 1990, p. 124). Such attempts amount to strategies designed to change organisational values by enshrining new values in custom and practice.

If we now have some idea of the way in which organisational values affect labour markets, we have yet to find out why organisational values (whether transmitted by strategy or by custom) affect labour markets. Once more, we will consider only the two most common explanations.

We begin with explanations which assume that labour market processes reflect the variety of ways in which firms can cohere as social groups. This explanation has two variants: in the first, labour market processes (for example recruitment practices) reflect an assumed need to *find* people who will fit into the organisation; in the second, labour market processes reflect an assumed need to *help or make* people fit in. Although, in practice, much research under both of these headings has tended to concentrate on strategies designed according to the organisational values of employers, it is clear from this initial description that there is room here for the consideration of custom and the organisational values of workers.

A great deal of research (for example, see Berg, 1981; Blackburn and Mann, 1979) reports that employers are less happy about hiring workers who are currently unemployed or have a history of intermittent employment. Sociologists need not believe that such histories are the effect of 'personal characteristics' (they may indeed be the product of previous labour market experience – see Norris, 1978b), but one of the most frequent explanations advanced to explain this pattern concerns the employers' fear that such employment (or, rather, unemployment) histories indicate that these workers do not have the attitudes appropriate to their organisation. Similarly, Ashton *et al.* (1990) find that, outside competitive and/or low-skill industries, labour costs do not appear to matter and that some employers do not even want to employ younger workers when they are free (as they have been when participating in the variety of training schemes for the young unemployed established by UK governments). In fact, the level of wages has little to do with their exclusion and Ashton *et al.* find that it is employers' judgements about the attitudes of younger workers that leads to exclusion:

In the lower segments they [employers] are more concerned that the recruits have the appropriate industrial discipline and attitude to work. This means that the same person can be ranked differently depending on the segment to which they are seeking entry. For example, a bright young person with a good record of educational achievement, will be ranked lowly by an employer recruiting a labourer or semi-skilled machinist as he or she will be seen as being overqualified and unlikely to settle in the job.

(Ashton *et al.*, 1990, p. 100)

Some of the questions of organisational values alluded to by researchers who have noted employers' concern with the attitudes of workers have been theorised using ideas of 'acceptability' versus 'suitability' or the concept of 'tacit skills'. Blackburn and Mann, in an early statement of a similar argument, conclude that:

... most workers are objectively capable of acquiring the skills necessary for most jobs; we estimate that 85 per cent of workers can do 95 per cent of jobs. Management would disagree with us; they are very concerned ... with a shortage of 'worker quality'. However, when we investigated what they meant by this, we found that they were worried, not about intelligence or manual dexterity, but about *worker co-operation.* Responsibility, stability, trustworthiness – such are the qualities by which (reasonably enough) they wish to select and promote. From the employer's point of view, the internal labour market allows workers to demonstrate these qualities (if they have them) over a number of years before they reach jobs where mistakes would matter.

(Blackburn and Mann, 1979, p. 280)

The distinction between 'acceptability' and 'suitability' is made by Jenkins (1983) in order to emphasise the importance assigned by both employers and existing employees to the personal characteristics of prospective recruits which will, it is believed, allow them to fit into the firm. Jenkins notes the importance of informal methods of recruitment in screening recruits for 'acceptability'. In similar fashion, Windolf and Wood find that in many German firms:

Management believes that through the social networks or through the internal labour market a highly reliable and motivated workforce can be found that is easy to integrate into the existing workforce whereas workers' representatives are interested in providing promotion opportunities or to shelter jobs from external competition. Recruitment through informal networks, so the argument goes, reduces potential conflicts because the applicants are more likely to be quickly socialised into the 'family of the firm'.

(Windolf and Wood, 1988, p. 201)

'Tacit skills' are uncertified abilities that make cooperative production easier or even possible, and employers use strategies to deal with problems of cooperation which have a variety of labour market effects (for example, see Manwaring, 1984). The main argument (although there are others) is that tacit skills are so valuable to employers that they are actually a big bit of what labour markets are for. So employers screen to pick up tacit skills and even use extended internal labour markets (EILMs) in which existing employees help to choose and even hire new recruits, to make sure that new recruits are trained in tacit skills.

The second common type of explanation as to why organisational values should affect labour markets is almost the reverse of the first. Here it is assumed that labour market processes reflect the way firms do *not* cohere as social groups, that is, explanation is found in the conflicts that occur between managers and workers, or even between different groups of workers. Again there are two variants: there are explanations that see labour market processes as reflecting the assumed need to avoid or cope with conflict, and there are explanations which see labour market processes as reflecting the assumed need to win conflicts.

Just as the arguments considered above can (all too often) be reduced to the idea that managers devise strategies to get workers to cooperate, so this second type of explanation can be reduced to the idea that managers devise strategies to get control over work and technology. In fact, both points can be made using the same material. Thus, it can be suggested (Maguire, 1986) that EILMs bring in recruits who resemble the existing workforce in that they will submit to management control, or that EILMs ensure that the existing workforce will do the job of controlling new recruits on management's behalf because they have been responsible for recruiting them. Another, similar argument suggests that EILMs represent the rewards due to existing workers who have been 'bought off' by management. Here we are not concerned so much with what the new recruits brought in by EILMs do, but with the existing workers' happiness with the balance of power (Jenkins *et al.*, 1983). Being allowed to arrange jobs for friends and relations, for instance, is believed to make workers content to let managers have control.

To summarise, according to this view there are three ways in which labour market processes reflect the conflicts (over control) which are believed to be endemic to capitalist production. Firstly, labour markets reflect managers' need to find workers who will submit to management control. Secondly, labour markets reflect managers' need for workers who can be relied on to exercise control on their behalf. Finally, labour markets reflect managers' attempts to control workers directly.

In the last category we already have the suggestion that EILMs buy off some groups of workers, but it is also suggested that workers can be bought off in other ways. For example, the radical economists discussed in Chapter 2 referred to different recruitment policies for different groups of workers created by management strategies of 'divide and rule'. A version of this argument is presented by Friedman (1978; see also Edwards, 1979) who distinguishes two types of control strategy, 'direct control' and 'responsible autonomy', which are used for 'peripheral' and 'core' workers respectively. Security of employment is an essential feature of responsible autonomy while insecurity (the expectation of lay-offs for example) is essential to direct control.

It seems that in this type of theory, everything that happens to labour market processes does so according to the will of management, but Friedman's thesis actually relies on effective 'worker resistance' to this will. Similarly, Windolf and Wood (1988) note that while EILMs, for example, may appear to work to managers' advantage they sometimes find that their organisational values dictate that they should set out to destroy EILMs in an effort to regain control over recruitment from the workforce. This sort of evidence can be incorporated into a theory which says labour market processes reflect conflicts, but the theory now refers to the effect on labour markets of the (more-or-less successful) attempts by workers to wrest control from management, or, at the least, to resist management control (see Rose, 1988).

For example, workers may seek to establish EILMs, or, as in the United States, to establish referral unions which managers rely on when they need to hire workers, as a strategy for extending (or resisting) control (also see Kumazawa and Yamada, 1989 on Japanese enterprise unions). Similarly, some writers refer to the labour market effects of struggles for control between workers and management, struggles in which the more strongly unionised workers tend to be the most successful. Where workers have more control we can expect 'vacancy competition' – something similar to Thurrow's job competition (see p. 104 above) – rather than wage competition (Schervish, 1981; Sørensen and Kalleberg, 1981).

Interestingly, Schervish uses this theory to analyse separations from employment. With vacancy competition, in what he calls 'high-capacity positions', workers have made themselves so invulnerable to market forces (irrespective of whether they are in a competitive sector or not) that they are less likely to lose their jobs – they may be temporarily laid off but they retain their jobs. Schervish also elaborates this analysis in order to explain why black workers in the United States suffer more unemployment, and concludes that this is the consequence of their patterns of employment rather than the direct result of discrimination (Schervish, 1981).

Similarly, several writers have commented on the sometimes

very effective worker resistance to changes in the labour process which are meant to put workers out of a job, but which do not do so because workers are able to retain control in spite of changes in technology or work organisation (see, for example, Lazonick, 1978; Rubery, 1978).[6] Finally, variations in labour market processes may result from conflicts between vying groups of workers intent on establishing their control in the workplace. Indeed, Burawoy (1979) argues that ILMs have the effect of turning tensions between capital and labour into tensions between workers.

We conclude this subsection as we did its predecessor. In practice fuller explanations of the complexity of modern labour markets must refer to more than organisational values. Such explanations also refer to economic values. Williamson (1975) points out that organisational values can be seen as a proxy for economic values. For example, bureaucratic organisation represents a means of achieving economic ends when market mechanisms have failed.

From a more orthodox economic point of view, Lindbeck and Snower (1987) question the importance of organisational values in the creation of stable employment by using their distinction between 'insiders' who are in employment and 'outsiders' who seek employment. In theory employers should be able to employ outsiders at lower wages than those presently paid to insiders, but in reality the behaviour of insiders will make it too costly for employers to recruit the outsiders at all. For example, insiders may threaten not to cooperate with outsiders, and outsiders may ask for higher wages to compensate for the harassment they fear the insiders will subject them to. Lindbeck and Snower conclude that 'there may exist no wage which both induces firms to hire outsiders *and* induces outsiders to work' (1987, p. 3).

Lindbeck and Snower's theory refers to the economic values of workers as much as those of employers, and insiders' actions are explained (at least in part) by their interest in keeping wages high. Similarly, the quotation from Windolf and Wood on p. 109 above referred to workers' interest in sheltering their jobs from competition. The theory of 'labour market shelters' (as developed by Freedman, 1976; see also Ashton, 1986) relies on the assumption that workers have economic reasons for wanting to be 'part of a firm', or for wanting any other type of shelter from competition – namely such shelters produce higher earnings, or, at the least, secure workers' incomes.

CONCLUSIONS

At the end of the last chapter we noted the crucial importance of finding the right questions to ask in order to create the theoretical diversity we needed to explain the complexity of modern labour markets. In the current chapter we posed a number of questions which were designed to produce this theoretical diversity. In the first place, we asked which social groups, relations and institutions arise on the basis of the economic division of labour. The three answers to this question which we considered gave us the three theoretical approaches – specialisation and co-operation, exploitation and conflict, legitimacy and the market – discussed in the first half of this chapter.

Since each of these approaches relies on a very different view of what is important in the economic division of labour, is it possible that they fit our requirement (see p. 80 above) that these should be complementary and not competing theories? At first glance this seems unlikely, but consider the second question asked in this chapter: what are the industrial values which arise with the economic division of labour which produces workers and jobs? We found three answers to this question (technical, organisational and economic values) but the crucial point is that all three theoretical approaches described earlier in the chapter contributed to the explanations in each category of industrial values. In practice, therefore, they provided complementary explanations of labour market diversity (see also Garnsey *et al.*, 1985).

The question of which explanation applies is, of course, always an empirical one, but this chapter has tended to suggest that when empirical labour market research identifies the appropriate theory for a particular case it may do so by finding out who has been able to make their construction of the labour market stick. For example, Norris (1978c) explains how the maintenance of paternalism may depend not simply on the size of enterprise concerned (it cannot be too big), but also on the extent to which the employer can dominate a local labour market, and on the limitation of access to employment opportunities outside the local labour market.

People organise themselves and conceive of themselves in different ways – as members of firms, as members of occupational groups, as capitalists or proletarians – in consequence of their roles in the economic division of labour. When they do this they establish different relationships to, and conceptions of, the labour market: industrial values, for example, vary between social groups. The task of research is to find out how these values vary and, most importantly, which values have the most influence on action. This can rarely be a simple question of finding out who has the power to make their values matter, however (Maurice *et al.*, 1986). We will return to these methodological problems in Chapter 6, but the present chapter has solved some other problems in a more satisfactory way.

In the preceding chapter we considered three categories of social values (people values, work values and market values) and then described three associated theories of the way in which labour markets work: discrimination, selection and matching. In the present chapter we have discussed industrial values (technical, organisational and economic) but we have not mentioned any associated theories of the way in which labour markets work. We have not been able to do this because discrimination, selection and matching describe the way in which industrial values as well as social values are put into effect as social processes. Since hiring and firing are always social processes the study of labour markets (or rather the sociology of labour markets) does not require further theories of the way in which labour markets work, although it does of course require some more-or-less prosaic distinctions, for example the distinction between formal and informal methods of recruitment, internal and external labour markets and so on.

Consider the following example. If you are the manager of a paternalist firm, you will have a particular idea about the sort of workers you want and even about how they should be hired. You may want them, for example, to fit in with the family of the firm and even the process of hiring (an EILM) can reflect this wish. Here the labour market is shaped by your organisational values, but how do you actually make your choice of recruits? There is no other basis for you to make this choice than discrimination, selection or matching. For example, you may consider that using people values will allow you to find the workers who fit your requirements (which are derived from your organisational values). In this case you discriminate in order to make the decisions which are necessary in order to achieve the goals set by industrial values. 'Discrimination' describes the way in which the labour market works when, in this example, the labour market reflects organisational values arising from the economic division of labour.

This is, of course, only a hypothetical example, and there is certainly no one-to-one correspondence between particular industrial values and particular ways of describing the way in which labour markets work: organisational values do not always lead to discrimination. Thus an employer who values rationalisation and bureaucracy may be more likely to prefer market values above people values and so will engage in processes of matching rather discrimination. Similarly, readers should not assume that employers who consider technical values important will always opt for selection, that is, for hiring and firing[7] based on work values.

Finally, this discussion allows us to conclude the account of discrimination given in the previous chapter. Readers will recall Banton's distinction between categorical and statistical discrimination. This was, indeed, as much an example of conceptual inflation as the usage of 'discrimination' which Banton sought to criticise, but here the concept that was being inflated was not discrimination but selection. In truth, what Banton means by 'statistical discrimination' is those actions of employers who are influenced by (industrial) technical values (not – social – work values), but the social process that he describes is nevertheless discrimination in the (non-inflated) sense described in Chapter 3. What makes it different (according to Banton, what makes it more 'rational' – a description we are now in a better position to dispute) is that it is discrimination informed by technical rather than by economic or organisational values. Similarly, the version of discrimination described by Jenkins (for example, 1983 and 1984) turns out to be discrimination informed by organisational values.

If they do nothing else, such distinctions serve to remind us of how catholic our studies must be if they are to bear fruit. If we limit sociological study to society we run the risk of errors, including conceptual inflation. For this reason we must also attend to economy and, in the following chapter, to polity.

NOTES

1. At this point conceptual inflation would lead us to argue that specialisation, including the special case of structural differentiation, is good for everyone because it is more efficient and it proceeds because it is more efficient (Rueschemeyer, 1986). It is more efficient to have the family specialising in the production of labour rather than the production of other commodities and it is more efficient to have companies specialising in the various production functions created in a complex division of labour. The 'proof' that this is better and more efficient can be found in the positive relationship between such specialisation and industrial development and in the presence of 'transitional' forms (domestic industry, for example, where the family has not yet abandoned its production function) in less advanced industrial societies.

2. The latter is the process which leads to exploitation: it turns raw materials, technology and labour into commodities and, hopefully, the capitalist's profit. Once exploitation actually occurs, and 'surplus' value is extracted from the labourers, it becomes a process of *valorisation*. But for any of this to happen the other (*labour*) process is also necessary. In the labour process, raw materials, technology and labour are combined to actually produce some*thing*.

3. Each of the subsections below will mention research on the demand side of the labour market and research on the supply side. In both cases we will consider work which addresses a variety of different levels of explanation, for example the level of industry and the level of the firm in discussions of labour demand. Readers should not confuse the idea of level with a social group, however. For example, we can say something important at the level of the firm even when we are not talking about the firm as an important social group.

4. Until very recent times much sociological interest in work and technology has been focused on male workers in manufacturing industry. Although this bias is no longer as noticeable, the legacy of the limitations of earlier work remains. In particular, critics of the focus on male manufacturing work argue that the legacy contributes to mistakes in sociologists' conception of skill.

5. A Marxist approach, however, might point out that multinational and

transnational corporations are so big that they can move production around the world to take advantage of cheaper labour wherever it is available. In this view (which relies on both organisational and economic values) the question of whether monopoly capital *will* take advantage of cheaper labour is not relevant. The point is that it *can*.

6. The impact of organisational values on technology receives little attention in the literature. Nevertheless, it is through work organisation *and* technology that organisational values affect labour markets.

7. In practice, employers in this position often leave the job of deciding who is to be made redundant to trade unions or, in the case of voluntary redundancy, to the workforce (see, for example, Harris *et al.*, 1987). Readers might like to note that, in terms of the distinctions explained in Chapter 3, voluntary redundancy amounts to a matching process for separation from employment. Relatedly, the principle of last-in-first-out leads to a process of selection (on the basis of a job value: the length of time in post) while seniority principles which refer to age rather than length of service lead to discrimination.

5

LABOUR MARKETS AND
THE STATE

Ideally this chapter would have been concerned with labour markets and polity as a whole, rather than with labour markets and the state. In the previous chapter analysis of social groups, institutions and relations was frequently reduced to analysis of the effects of the actions of (dominant) employers – and to their institutions, and their relations with others – but the present chapter is even more one-dimensional. To date, analysis of aspects of polity other than the state have been, for the most part, neglected in the large literature on the subject. While making every effort to refer to wider aspects of polity whenever this is possible, we have therefore no option but to concentrate our attention on labour markets and the state.

For the purposes of this book, however, we do not have to take into account all sociological writing on labour markets and the state. No attempt is made below to do justice to the large volume of literature which is, of course, valuable in other ways even if it does not address the narrower concerns of the sociology of labour markets as defined in this book. But, as before, it is the definition of the sociology of labour markets employed here that provides the criteria of relevance.

Firstly, we will not attend to political differences in name only. For example, where labour markets differ between countries which share the same form of government, and administrations of the same political leanings, then labour market differences do not arise from differences in polity but from factors already considered under the headings of society and economy. We are interested in the content rather than the form of political difference, and political boundaries are not significant in themselves.

Secondly, we will not refer to cases where there may be genuine political differences which coincide with labour market differences, but the real cause of labour market difference lies elsewhere (in society and economy). Thirdly, we will not discuss political differences which are indirect causes of labour market difference. That is, we will try to avoid referring to cases where polity causes differences in society and economy which then cause labour market differences.

The distinction between direct and indirect political effects on labour markets is always difficult to draw. In what follows the indirect effects of broad economic policy and policy on trade and industry are excluded along with more obviously indirect influences like housing policy. Of course these aspects of government policy can affect labour markets, but this influence is judged indirect when compared, for example, with the more direct influence of government policy in the fields of education and training on labour markets. Nevertheless, many readers may feel that the exclusion of indirect influences could be carried too far, and the criteria of relevance will be ignored in one important case in order to include the strictly indirect influence on labour markets of state (and state agencies) acting as employers.

The question of public sector employment might have arisen in the previous chapter and, indeed, readers have already been introduced to some of the thinking that lies behind analyses of the effect of public sector employment on labour markets. Nevertheless, it makes sense to investigate public sector employment in the present chapter because it is in the labour market effects of this type of employment that we might expect to find evidence that the state deserves attention in its own right. If there were nothing of interest to the sociology of labour markets in public sector employment in itself, we would still be wise to discuss it because it is likely that we will discover the influence of the state (and perhaps even of other aspects of polity) here.

We have now suggested that there are two ways in which the state can have a relevant influence on labour markets: through the effects of government policy (as enforced by state organisations and through legislation) and through public sector employment. Simply in order to avoid repetition, examples of the former will provide the bulk of the illustrative material in the second half of the chapter, while public sector employment will receive more attention in the first half.

It is appropriate to describe the chapter as falling into two 'halves' because this chapter is designed to answer two questions. In the first half of the chapter we ask if there is any evidence that the state has an independent and important effect on labour markets. In order to answer this question, we deal firstly with some (general) empirical evidence and then with some theoretical material of a kind which has become familiar in earlier chapters. In the second half of the chapter we ask whether we need any new explanations (explanations which are noticeably different from those used in Chapters 3 and 4) to account for this independent effect.

THE STATE AND THE WORKINGS OF LABOUR MARKETS

We begin by considering empirical evidence which suggests that the state does have an independent and important effect. Before we consider the effects of states on the workings of labour markets, we will briefly consider the role of states in the making of · modern labour markets and in the structure of labour markets.

We have already seen in Chapter 4 how, in the early history of industrialisation, for example in Europe, labour markets had an apparently difficult birth. In some cases these problems were resolved with caesarean sections performed by those who had a monopoly of legal violence. The biggest problem was the reluctance of the potential free labourers to sell their labour, and a combination of physical and legal compulsion by the state helped to bring modern labour markets into being because it created the missing (or reluctant) supply side of the labour market (see also Miles, 1987).

Varieties of forced labour had, of course, been around for a long time, but in the cases that concern us here unfree labour was a substitute for inadequate free labour. Where unfree labour (slaves, indentured labourers, debt-peons, pauper apprentices and so on) was used in the private sector, it required the legislative connivance of the state and sometimes relied, in addition, on the state's monopoly of legitimate physical force. On occasion, this unfree labour (of prisoners and of paupers for example) was the property of the state (Melossi and Pavarini, 1981).

An examination of the political debates about slavery or child labour might tell us rather more about the relationship between broader aspects of polity and the making of labour markets, but at least we can draw the simple conclusion that – through its monopoly of legitimate physical force – the state has helped to create modern labour markets. We now turn to labour market structure.

Some jobs and organisations, and even whole occupations and industries, would not exist if it were not for the addition to the division of labour of public sector employment. For example, there would certainly be less social workers employed in the United States and the United Kingdom if there were none employed by the public sector. As far as industries are concerned, consider the accelerated decline of some branches of primary and manufacturing industry in the United Kingdom and in some countries in Eastern Europe beginning in the 1980s. Some of these industries almost disappeared when they ceased to be part of the public sector (or even when this was merely threatened), suggesting that they owed their very existence to forms of state ownership. In similar fashion we might also consider the changes in numbers of personnel in the armed forces (and employees in defence industries) planned by many countries at the end of the 1980s.

While it is true to say that some jobs, occupations and even industries would not exist were they not included in the public sector, it can also be suggested that some jobs, occupations and industries might exist were it not for the state. Prohibition in the United States, for example, affected the structure of American labour markets. Radical thinkers of the 'new right' in Britain (also see Bacon and Eltis, 1976) have made this point in a more general way: government 'interference' in the economy – including public ownership – prevents job creation by the private sector.

Variations in labour market structure are clearly related to differences in the extent of public sector employment. Differences in the extent of public sector employment between countries were obvious for most of the second half of the twentieth century when Eastern European states, in particular, had almost all production under their control. But such differences also existed within countries. In the United Kingdom for example, every 'local labour market' contains within it some public sector jobs (teachers, police officers and so on), but the proportion of public sector jobs will also vary between local labour markets. For example, some local labour markets are (or were) dominated by a single public sector employer (see, for example, Fevre, 1989b).

Clearly the effect of public sector employment on the structure of labour markets can help to explain labour market change as well as international or regional variations. We have already noted the decline of certain industries in Eastern Europe and the United Kingdom for example. In very general terms, the twentieth century has (so far) seen an increase in state sector employment in centralised economies and in some mixed economies (both in Europe and elsewhere) followed by rapid – but not yet universal – decline (especially in Europe).

Differences in the nature and extent of public sector employment over time and space produce differences at the level of social groups and relations. In the United Kingdom, there are trade unions (e.g. the National Association of Local Government Officers, the Civil and Public Servants Association), professional associations (e.g the National Association of Probation Officers, The British Association of Social Workers) and qualifications (e.g Civil Service entry examinations or the Certificate of Qualification in Social Work) which owe their existence to public sector employment. But does this really matter – we have some new names but what could really be different about public sector employment as far as labour markets are concerned? For example, there may be more service-sector jobs in the labour market than there would have been without state employment; there may be more clerical workers too (with their own unions, qualifications and so on); but does this mean we need to employ anything more than the existing society and economy analysis when trying to understand these things? What is to prevent us from using the analysis already applied to the (private) service sector, to private sector clerical workers and so on?

According to most writers we cannot rely on society and economy analyses because the effect of public sector employment on labour markets cannot be fully explained in terms of the theories and explanations offered in earlier chapters: state industries and organisations do not necessarily have the same effects on labour markets as non-state industries and firms. In other words, the state makes a difference to the way in which labour markets work.

Differences in the way labour markets work may be associated with political differences, of which the most obvious examples are differences between forms of government and between administrations of different political persuasions. In the latter case, the political differences may even be minor party-political ones between local administrative regions of the same state. In the former case, for example, one sort of labour market may be concentrated in states with a particular form of government such as single-party rule, while most labour markets of another sort are located in states which espouse multiparty democracies. Ashton (1986) describes the less extreme case of political difference between the United States and the United Kingdom which is none the less of considerable significance for the workings of labour markets (for further comparative material see Fulcher, 1987 who provides details on Sweden).

Ashton notes the more collectivist and comprehensive traditions of policy in the United Kingdom and the larger, and more decentralised, nature of the US state which together produce differences in policy-making and policy-implementation in the two countries (also see Ashton, 1988b for a comparison of the United Kingdom and Canada). He finds that, along with differences in the role of labour unions in the United Kingdom and the United States, differences in policy help to explain differences in the way labour markets work on either side of the Atlantic.

A history of greater regulation in the United Kingdom has created 'base-line' conditions for hiring and firing which do not exist in the United States although, in consequence of some deregulation and of structural change, a growing number of workers in the United Kingdom do not benefit from this regulation of hiring and firing (for an alternative view of the United Kingdom see Craig *et al.*, 1985; for further European material see the collection of papers in *Labour and Society*, 1987). As a result, hiring and firing practices for permanent full-time workers in the United Kingdom are broadly similar, and the major labour market division lies between permanent full-time employees, who receive protection from trade unions and the state, and temporary and part-time workers who receive much less protection.

According to Ashton, labour markets in the United States exhibit many more divisions than those in the United Kingdom as a result, in part, of decentralised institutional regulation. In consequence, a larger proportion of workers in the United States are likely to experience some unemployment:

> the cost of that greater security for those in work in Britain is that those in the more insecure jobs share a greater burden of unemployment and find it more difficult to re-enter work once they are unemployed. The result is that a higher proportion are confined to the ranks of the unemployed. In the USA the evidence suggests that that insecurity is shouldered by a larger section of the labour force, who find it easier to re-enter work but for whom the insecurity of the labour market is a more serious threat than it is in Britain.
>
> (Ashton, 1986, p. 104)

Ashton's explanation of the differences between labour markets in the United States and the United Kingdom in terms of the role of the state does not refer simply to differences in state regulation of hiring and firing, however. Ashton also refers to the characteristics of public sector employment in the United States and the United Kingdom because the workings of labour markets are affected by differences in (for example, the extent of) public sector employment as well as by differences in regulatory policy.

In common with many other writers, Ashton contrasts the security of public sector employment with the insecurity of employment in the private sector. If, *unlike* Ashton, we over-simplify this point of view, we can make a distinction between public and private employment which assumes that workers in the public sector are better off and get more of what they want. This state of affairs exists because lack of competition is assumed to make workers more powerful and managers less worried about conceding to their demands. As a result, workers in the public sector may get higher wages, but they will certainly have much more job security. They will probably have an internal labour market (ILM) which provides prospects of advancement and perhaps even the employment tenure which is still believed to exist in the United Kingdom Civil Service.

In the United Kingdom, at least, public sector ILMs certainly do appear to differ (at least in kind) from those in the private sector.

Blackburn and Mann describe private-sector ILMs as neither uniform nor predictable: 'Most promotion practices are unclear and so the entering worker can rarely be in a position to predict his "career" within the firm' (Blackburn and Mann, 1979, p. 279). By way of contrast, public sector ILMs tend to have (very few) ports of entry which give access to a variety of different jobs and occupations, and to sometimes apparently limitless possibilities for advancement. As far as job security is concerned, Ashton concludes – as do several other writers – that public sector employment is a source of 'labour market shelters': public sector employees benefit from the fact that their employer is not engaged in competition, but they are themselves protected from the stiff winds of competition in the labour market.

Ashton (1986) does not, however, recommend that we see all public sector employees as the beneficiaries of labour market shelters or gilt-edged ILMs. Such a conclusion would, indeed, make little sense to the many unemployed workers who were once public sector employees in the United Kingdom or in the countries of Eastern Europe. In similar vein, there is a great deal of evidence to suggest that even those who manage to keep their jobs in the public sector are not always better off than workers in the private sector.

For example, Brooks (1975) described the recruitment (from the 1950s) of workers from the Caribbean to work in public sector transport in the United Kingdom, because there were so many unfilled vacancies in this part of the public sector. While these jobs were secure and sometimes offered access to ILMs, the level of wages was too low to attract indigenous workers. A similar pattern emerged elsewhere in the UK public sector, notably in the National Health Service. More recently, public sector workers in the United Kingdom have largely failed to achieve wage increases which match those won by workers in the private sector, and in some categories of public sector employment the problem of unfilled vacancies (caused by low wages) reappeared in the late 1980s even though unemployment remained high. Thus over 5 per cent of teaching posts in the old inner-London boroughs were vacant in 1990.

According to the simple theory of the labour market effects of public sector employment explained above, this sort of thing should not happen. The funding from tax revenue which some state organisations enjoy means that profits need not enter into the deliberations of these organisations, and decisions (including those which affect labour markets) have some other basis than the one which is (arguably) the most familiar to private sector employers. It is argued that the state sector is insulated from competitive pressures and therefore the labour markets it affects look, and work, in a different way to those which depend on private sector jobs. That there is evidence (ILMs and so on) for this theory is not in dispute; but there is dispute about whether this is all the evidence and (especially) whether the evidence is being understood in the only possible way. In the simple absence-of-competition theory it is assumed that the state does not have to resist workers' pressure to insulate themselves from the labour market in a variety of ways. The state can afford to give in to workers' demands to be sheltered from competition because the state as employer is itself sheltered from competition.

We have already seen, however, that as far as some public sector jobs are concerned, the state sector is not so much outside competition, but below it. Such jobs might still be technically classed as labour market shelters, if they remain a part of ILMs for example, but wages are so low that most workers appear to reject them. The workers who occupy them have 'sheltered' from competition with other workers by taking the jobs nobody else wants! Thus, we found examples of public sector jobs that were less attractive than jobs in the private sector, and, indeed, we found evidence of unfilled public sector vacancies.

There is a fundamental problem with a theory which refers to differences in labour market competition which are caused by the state's own peculiar relationship to economic competition. Take the bus drivers, nurses and teachers mentioned above: we might have expected pressure by these workers to make their jobs better – there is no obvious reason why British bus drivers in the 1950s, or teachers in the 1990s, should exert less pressure on their employers – so why were their efforts unrewarded? Perhaps there is more going on in the public sector than the state (as employer) giving in to workers because it is, itself, insulated from competitive pressures? Indeed, are we even correct to explain the existence of more attractive public sector jobs in these terms?

Even if we agree that there are labour market shelters, or something like them, in the public sector, and that public sector jobs are in some respects better than others, such characteristics are not necessarily simply the result of worker pressure. A more satisfactory explanation can be found in work which derives from the theories of Thurrow (see p. 104 above) and which is to be found in many of the chapters in Berg (1981), but also see Schervish (1983) and the commentary in Ashton (1986).

In this view, the existence of 'good' jobs in the public sector (gilt-edged ILMs and so on) indicates that the state does not use wages in the way it is supposed to. Public sector employers do not force workers to compete by offering to work for lower wages but make them compete, for example by lining up in queues, for vacancies. Workers cannot jump a queue for a gilt-edged ILM by offering to work for a lower wage.

The theory of wage versus vacancy competition (and its more sophisticated variants) also explains the anomalous evidence. If labour market shelters are not the result of workers' pressure (to which public sector employers succumb merely because they have no compelling reasons to resist), then we are no longer surprised to find that such shelters offer little protection to some workers, for example those ex-public employees who find themselves out of work. The theory of wage versus vacancy competition also explains the unattractive nature of some of the jobs that remain in the public sector.

Just as the state (as employer) does not respond to workers' economic signals in the form of wage rates, so the state does not use these wage signals itself. A private sector firm might be more likely to increase wages if it had unfilled vacancies, but the public sector employer simply puts up with these vacancies. Similarly, public sector employers will not use wage signals (alone, or even at all) when they want to dispense with workers. Here workers are forced to engage in a process of job competition in order to stay in work. In sum, public sector employment is not sheltered from competition altogether. There is, instead, a different kind of competition: vacancy or job competition co-exists with, and perhaps even dominates, wage competition.

Finally, we turn to some related work on states and labour markets in Eastern Europe, in particular to work on the Eastern European country which was reforming at a greater pace than the others in the 1980s: Hungary. This work derives, in large part, from Kornai's analysis of the 'shortage economies' of Eastern

Europe (Kornai, 1980; also see Burawoy and Lukács, 1989) and from Kornai's later discussion of the shift from bureaucratic to market mechanisms in these economies (for a discussion of this work see Neumann, 1989). Kornai's ideas provide the theoretical basis for Stark's study of ILMs in Hungarian state-owned enterprises. Stark concludes that these ILMs exist to create market mechanisms which allow Hungarian enterprises to cope with the *bureaucratic* uncertainty which is endemic in a shortage economy (Stark, 1986).

Neumann (1989) finds that Stark overplays the market character of Hungarian ILMs. Neumann prefers, instead, to emphasise 'the social character of the bargaining parties' informal system of rules' (Neumann, 1989, p. 85). Nevertheless, there is much in Stark's analysis which is interesting and useful. Stark contends that ILMs are established in conditions of uncertainty. In a capitalist economy ILMs establish bureaucratic rules which allow firms to cope with market uncertainty. In a socialist economy ILMs establish market mechanisms which allow firms to cope with bureaucratic uncertainty. In order to cope with unexpected demands (for increased production) made by the bureaucracy, the socialist firm holds on to labour and provides ILMs for its most valued workers. These ILMs do not work to the advantage of Hungarian enterprises because they provide shelters from competition for the valued workers, but because they offer them the (rare) opportunity of limited participation in the market (Stark, 1986, p. 496). Stark concludes that:

To mitigate the effects of supply bottlenecks or to circumvent the obstacles of centrally imposed wage regulations, neither workers nor managers have an interest in the routinization of internal systems of classification. On the contrary, the strategy of an internal labor market, in this case, is to create some space relatively insulated from the bureaucratic principles that govern the planned economy.

(Stark, 1986, p. 503)

We began this discussion of the state and labour markets with a simple theory which suggested that state employment was different because the state was not subject to competitive pressures; state employment was therefore less competitive. We then considered a more complex theory which referred to a different kind of competition in public sector employment. We have concluded the discussion with an account of research which suggests that in countries where most employment is in the public sector, the bureaucratic uncertainty engendered by the state can produce market responses from individual enterprises. Indeed, it has even been suggested that ILMs in these countries are more competitive than those in the private sector in countries with comparatively little public sector employment (but see Neumann, 1989). This is certainly a long way from the simple absence-of-competition theory but it nevertheless provides dramatic confirmation that states can have an important and independent effect on the way in which labour markets work.

SOCIOLOGICAL THEORIES OF THE STATE

We now turn from empirical evidence of an independent role for the state which is of significance in the sociology of labour markets, to complementary *theoretical* evidence of the significance of the state. We know from earlier chapters that basic consensus of opinion – for example, on the importance of the social division of labour or social hierarchy, on the importance of exchange or the economic division of labour – is characteristic of labour market sociology. We also know that this consensus comes under threat as soon as we ask what important social groups, institutions and relations arise on the basis of that part of the analysis that is agreed. The diversity of opinion which this question produces is, to repeat, vitally necessary to labour market sociology. We must therefore try to follow the model of earlier chapters – basic consensus followed by theoretical diversity – in the present one.

In this chapter, politics might play a similar (methodological) role to that played by exchange in the previous chapter. Sociologists are generally agreed that polity brings to our attention new groups, relations and institutions (without polity we have no governments, political parties, or lobbying for example). In this case, polity is not just influencing labour markets by providing new conduits for other influences already discussed. There is more to political parties than social class, for example (Weber, 1948).

We do not, however, have the opportunity to produce the

theoretical diversity we need in this way, because, as noted above, sociologists have concentrated their attention on the state. We cannot ask about theoretical divergence on the basis of different opinions about what important social groups, institutions and relations arise on the basis of that part (the politics part) of the analysis that is agreed, because there is little divergence of sociological opinion about what is important about politics (as far as labour markets are concerned). There is, instead, general agreement that the important thing about politics is the state.

There is, therefore, little point in including a section on social groups, relations and institutions (the method followed in Chapters 3 and 4) and we must make do with a discussion of sociological theories of the state instead. Differences of socio-logical opinion will give us at least a semblance of the theoretical diversity which we will need to explain complex modern labour markets. These differences closely resemble those discussed in the previous chapter and readers will soon recognise the continuity of theoretical traditions between the discussions below and those on pp. 85–96 above. In each of these discussions, we consider varying sociological attempts to explain why the state comes about and, therefore, to explain what the state is about. Explanations which refer to each of the three different approaches described here will be discussed in the second half of this chapter (when we consider polity values).

We begin with a view which is very often adopted by governments – in the guise of 'corporatism' – as well as by social scientists (see, for example, MacInnes, 1987; cf. Fulcher, 1987). According to this view the state is able to take a more rational, longer-term approach to problems of economic development than those who are involved directly in industry and commerce. While taking the interests of both workers and employers into account, and to some extent being guided by them, the state alone can engage in long-term planning for a country's economy and, in partnership with the representatives of workers and employers, can develop policies to achieve these long-term aims. Since the state can do more than respond to short-term economic pressures, the effects of its policies may well be less cruel, and (in the longer term) more efficient, than the effects of the somewhat anarchic actions of workers and employers who cannot plan beyond the short term and are buffeted by economic pressures.

In this view, the creation of ILMs and assurances of job security in public sector employment may well make good sense in the longer term; they can be seen, for example, as ways of finding the best workers for the jobs on offer, or as ways of ensuring cooperation from those workers who are recruited. But the economic policies of the state do not always address such narrow concerns. Thus, if future economic prosperity depends upon the social effect of current economic policy, the state may wish to take the social effects of this policy into account. This thinking is a major part of the rationale behind the 'Social Charter' proposed for the member countries of the European Community. Two other examples follow.

Firstly, when planning public employment, states are able to take into account the social effects of industrial location decisions. They also do this when subsidising or directing employment in the private sector too, of course. In either case the state can ensure that jobs are created where they are most needed and therefore ease the path of economic and industrial change. By the same token, states can do something to ameliorate the uneven regional effects of reductions in employment brought about by economic and industrial change (in either the public or private sectors) by providing financial aid to the supernumerary workers, retraining and relocation subsidies.

The United Kingdom is not usually considered as corporatist as many other European countries, even though it is often seen as more corporatist than the United States (compare Ashton, 1986 to MacInnes, 1987 who thinks the United Kingdom is not corporatist enough). But even in the United Kingdom the state has been historically responsible for creating large numbers of secure (and highly paid) jobs for men in regions with high unemployment; for creating jobs for women in regions where women had very few employment opportunities at all; and (with help from the European Community) for high levels of public expenditure in areas which have been adversely affected by economic and industrial change (Fevre, 1987).

The second example concerns equal opportunities in the public sector. Since the 1960s, there has been growing emphasis in federal policy in the United States on the regulation of labour markets in order to promote equal opportunities. For example, contract compliance policies which force government contractors to follow equal opportunities guidelines have been far more rigorously enforced in the United States than in the United Kingdom (which is supposedly more corporatist). This different way of running labour markets is thought to get the best workers for the job but is nevertheless seen as socially responsible too (although it is, of course, the result of politics: DiPrete and Grusky, 1990).

If the first approach can be summarised by saying that industrialism will go better if the state is both involved and has an independent role, the second approach says that capitalism will go better if the state is involved but has a dependent role. There are, of course, a variety of (more-or-less sophisticated) Marxist theories of the state, but the basic idea is that the state is a tool of the capitalist class.

For example, it can be argued that when most Western European countries encouraged the immigration of large numbers of workers from less developed countries in the second half of the twentieth century, they did so because the governments in each of the receiving countries could see that large numbers of poor migrant workers, members of the 'reserve army of labour', would help capitalists to increase the general level of exploitation. Some of these migrants (including the majority of workers who migrated to the United Kingdom from the Caribbean, East Africa and the Indian subcontinent) were, or became, citizens of the countries to which they migrated, but very few of them benefited from equal opportunities policies. According to a particular Marxist view, equal opportunities were not extended to the migrants because this would make their labour more expensive (they would no longer be members of the reserve army of labour in fact – see pp. 90–2 above) and this would not serve the interests of capitalists (see, for example, Castles and Kosack 1973; Sivanandan, 1982).

Finally, we turn to the concerns of Weberian theory: the legitimation of authority and bureaucratic forms of organisation. To continue with the example of equal opportunities policies, Weberian theory will clearly see such policies as the outcome of attempts to extend bureaucratic organisation and, particularly, to extend rational–legal–universal authority. If the state steps in to enforce equal opportunities in the labour market, it does it to make the market more effective in meeting the criteria that make markets acceptable ways of distributing people and jobs (see pp. 93–6 above: markets are accepted because they are believed to be rational–legal–universal mechanisms).

In this view, equal opportunity policies are an attempt to make markets work as they are supposed to and so to maintain their legitimacy. They will be most rigorously enforced in the public sector since the state is conspicuously more bureaucratic, and more concerned with questions of rational–legal–universal authority, than private sector employers can be. It is for this reason, we might conclude, that public sector employment has afforded proportionately more jobs to black workers in the United Kingdom for example (cf. p. 125 above where we discussed the difficulties of filling public sector vacancies, for example in transport and health). Furthermore, DiPrete and Grusky (1990) conclude that, while bureaucratic personnel policies in general have helped to bring about equal opportunities in the United States, the actions of governments have had a proportionately greater effect.

Dworkin (1980) and Glazer (1980) have debated the extent to which equal opportunities policies in United States have impeded or created 'efficiency' and 'fairness'. According to one interpretation of Weberian theory this is beside the point. We cannot hope to say whether rational–legal–universal mechanisms produce real efficiency or real fairness, but only to explain that it is in pursuit of these aims that such mechanisms are adopted. Thus Civil Service recruitment procedures may be generally thought more likely to operate according to rational–legal–universal principles but there may be no general agreement on whether these procedures are either fair or efficient.

A similar point can be made in respect of the corporatist approach to economic management discussed above. Some sociologists appear to believe that a state which favours corporatism has simply discovered the truth of the matter: it operates in the way that a state in an established industrial society is supposed to. From a Weberian viewpoint (for example, Goldthorpe, 1984), it is not the truth that the corporatist state has discovered but a mode of operation that is acceptable for political authority in a social democracy (cf. Fulcher, 1987; see also Offe, 1985).

The same conclusion can be reached by a different route if we consider recent shifts in policy in the United Kingdom and similar, but much bigger, changes in the countries of Eastern Europe (in some cases directly modelled on the UK experience in the 1980s). After the collapse of centralised planning in these countries, governments were bent on reducing the size of the public sector (through reductions in employment as well as through privatisation) and on changing the nature of public sector employment. To a greater or lesser extent (depending on the country in question) there followed a reduction in job security and in the coverage of ILMs in the public sector.[1]

These labour market effects followed a change in political ideology (also see Therborn, 1985, and Goldthorpe, 1984). As long as sociologists do not assume that one particular political ideology is superior (more fair, more efficient) to all others we are left to conclude that the behaviour of the state is contingent upon ideological influences as well as, or instead of, reflecting a hidden (but sensible) agenda for all states in established industrial societies or reflecting the needs of capitalists. But if we accept this conclusion we are immediately faced with another problem: what is the mechanism whereby political ideology influences labour markets? The answer to this question (amongst others) can be found in what remains of this chapter since it is through polity *values* that political ideology affects labour markets.

POLITY VALUES

We have found that, on theoretical as well as empirical grounds, the state 'matters' as far as labour markets are concerned. We have also discovered the basis of the different types of sociological theory we will need to explain the labour market effects of the state, but to what should these theories be applied?

Let us consider the question of public sector employment. As in the previous chapter, we have discovered that the actions of employers are informed by something else, something more, than *economic* values. For example, it was implicit in the conclusion to the discussion of public sector employment that employers in the public sector were so little influenced by economic values that they could, on the one hand, bear excessive wages and/or workers' tenure of jobs, and, on the other hand, could put up with unfilled vacancies.

It is not impossible to retain a place for economic values in the face of such evidence. We might argue, for example, that differences in the funding of employment in the public sector lead employers to take a longer-term view. Thus the different signals used by public sector employers (ILMs instead of higher pay) follow from their more secure, but less generous, funding. Yet explanations of this kind seem to be secondary, and almost spurious (as far as our present purposes are concerned), when we remember that public sector jobs appear to change with changes in polity (for example, in forms of government or even just administrations). Jobs which were once more attractive than most can become much less desirable as a result of this political change. Political change can even lead to the abolition of ILMs in public sector jobs.

Clearly, the technical and organisational values discussed in the previous chapter can be used to supplement an explanation of the effect of public sector employment on labour markets in terms of economic values, but even this would not be sufficient to explain the unique contribution of the public sector. A comprehensive explanation requires that we also consider polity values.

We now consider three categories of polity values which are relevant to labour markets (there are lots of other polity values too, of course). That these really are polity values will become clear below. We are not considering 'state values' but values which are first introduced into the political realm before the state can use them as a guide to action. We will look, in each case, at how these values influence the state as employer and (mostly) the state as authority and legislator. We will not, however, be able to ignore other sorts of values altogether and there will be some brief 'interdisciplinary' discussion of the type encountered in Chapter 4 (for example, under the heading of unemployment I will mention Marxist theories of economic as well as polity values).

The independent focus of polity – something which is not a focus, does not come into the analysis of values in our earlier discussions of society and economy – is on unemployment, employment, and education and training. For the state (and for wider polity) unemployment *in the polity*, employment *in the polity*, and education and training *in the polity* become values which then affect labour markets in a way that they never could through society and economy. In consequence, these could never be the ends (in themselves) of social actions considered in the society and economy analyses above, whereas they can be with analysis at the level of polity.[2] It is not, for instance, the workers' (or employers'?) fear of redundancy, or fear of not getting a job, but unemployment in the whole country (or supranational region in the case of political organisations above the level of the state) that we wish to bring into our explanation. When we refer to unemployment, employment, and education and training values, we mean that these ideas are sources of decisions (state decisions in most of the examples below) which affect labour markets: for instance, the state brings them to hiring and firing either through its role as an employer or as the political authority.[3]

Readers will probably anticipate that the polity values considered below frequently come to attention as social problems. They will shortly see that in several cases unemployment has come to the attention of the state as a social problem. Similarly, aspects of employment and of education and training have often been considered social problems. There is, however, no hard and fast rule here. In the United Kingdom education and training remained active polity values even before the explosion of public concern about education and training in the late 1980s which put them in the category of social problem.

One final point to be made before beginning the discussion of polity values concerns the organisation of the three subsections below. To avoid repetition, each subsection will perform a different function. The discussion of unemployment is intended to demonstrate how polity values become a societal concern, and latterly a state concern, and then (briefly) to show how such values can change. This subsection will say little about the mechanisms whereby labour markets are affected by polity values, or about the effects themselves, since these are exemplified in the other subsections.

The subsection on employment will illustrate the mechanisms which affect (through the resulting behaviour of workers and employers) labour markets, and includes a detailed discussion of examples of employment values in practice. Finally, the discussion of education and training will give confirmation of the effect of polity values on labour markets by showing how this conclusion can be reached from a variety of theoretical perspectives. Illustrations will be drawn from each of the sociological theories of the state discussed earlier in this chapter. This final subsection concludes by reiterating the point (also made in the previous chapter) that we have been discussing the labour market effects of *values* and not of facts or circumstances.

Unemployment

Accounts of state involvement in the creation of the idea of unemployment and of how unemployment came to be seen as the state's concern are available for the United States (Ashton, 1986; Keyssar, 1986; and see also Piore, 1987), France (Salais *et al.*, 1986) and the United Kingdom (Ashton, 1986; Keane and Owens, 1986). Keane and Owens' account of the idea of unemployment in the United Kingdom, for example, tells how unemployment came to be seen as a social problem when peoples' ways of making ends meet outside the labour market began to disappear during industrialisation, and when employers realised that such alternatives might be discouraged anyway since they threatened industrial discipline. Keane and Owens also describe the process whereby compulsory education and the exclusion of women from the Factory System led to most households having only one or two 'bread-winners': if one of these members lost employment the consequences for the household were serious.

As far as the state was concerned, the British Treasury had always said there was nothing the state could or should do about unemployment but this stance was modified in the 1840s and, later, in the 1850s and 1860s, when 'public works' were funded to relieve destitution resulting from a variety of causes such as the Irish famine. According to Keane and Owens, the state was also affected by increased public attention and sympathy for the 'deserving unemployed' and by trade union involvement from the 1880s which increased the fear of the (social and) political consequences of unemployment.

Unemployment was on the agenda of the UK government by the first half of the twentieth century but it was still supposed that state interference would make matters worse. The Liberal

Government at the start of the century was only interested in alleviating, and not in curing, the problem, but the Second World War showed that full employment could be achieved through state intervention. During the war the state was engaged in full-scale regulation and mobilisation; and every market, but especially the labour market, was subject to state control (including financial control). The result was full male employment and higher living standards.

In the United Kingdom unemployment was no longer seen as inevitable, and Keane and Owens describe the guiding principles of a new, post-war consensus which were summarised by Beveridge (1944). First, equality in the distribution of income and wealth was a government goal. Second, this would be achieved by way of full employment for men and a system of social security. Full employment would be achieved by stimulating growth and hence private sector employment, and also by government regulation of the economy involving the expansion of the public sector where necessary.

There is no need to dwell on the unmistakable evidence of labour market effects which followed the changes described by Keane and Owens. The behaviour of workers and employers was affected in fundamental ways by the adoption of unemployment as a value to guide the actions of the state. The hiring and firing behaviour of employers, for example, is affected by their view of the adequacy of state welfare for the unemployed. Similarly, the labour market literature is full of references to the effect of welfare policies on the labour market behaviour, for example the job-search behaviour, of workers, and a number of intriguing concepts like 'income replacement ratios' (Morris and Dilnot, 1982) and 'reservation wages' (see, for example, Fallon and Verry, 1988) have been used to help us to explain these effects.

We have seen how the state – in this case the British state – was involved in the creation of unemployment values and we have seen how unemployment came to be seen as the state's concern. We can conclude this chapter by briefly showing how these values are reconstructed at times of crisis (see Keyssar, 1986; Piore, 1987; Salais *et al.*, 1986).

Let us return to the work of Keane and Owens (1986). We left their account with a description of the political consensus which prevailed in the United Kingdom at the end of the Second World

War. The consensus they describe lasted for three decades but broke down in the 1970s when, Keane and Owens say, it became clear that the full employment welfare state which had been described by Beveridge entailed a compromise between the interests of capital and labour. The state had no alternative but to conclude that the compromise had been struck in favour of labour and in a way which threatened the economy. The state was therefore obliged to dismantle aspects of the full employment welfare state.[4]

For present purposes, the important point to note about this change in policy is not historical but theoretical. Keane and Owens go on to describe what amounts to a reconstruction of the idea of unemployment in a time of crisis: there were changes in the way the blame for unemployment was apportioned, in the level and administration of welfare benefits, and changes in how unemployment was counted. Other research, especially the work of French social scientists, confirms that this is not a unique experience and, moreover, that it is one from which we can draw important conclusions.

Piore (1987) reports the research of Salais *et al.* (1986) which shows how, in France, the general system of unemployment insurance was created as a permanent institution because of two temporary effects; and how it was created as a particular model of the unemployment experienced by workers who depended on large, manufacturing enterprises for work. Workers responded by structuring their employment behaviour on the large enterprise model. Similarly, in the late twentieth century, another crisis brought about a reconstruction of unemployment in several countries. Unemployment welfare in the United States and Western Europe was meant to be self-financing but unemployment in the 1980s was outside the normal distribution (with which the system could cope) (Piore, 1987, p. 1848). The reconstruction that followed is well-illustrated by changes in the methods of compiling official unemployment statistics.

In the United Kingdom governments made thirty changes in the official methods of counting the unemployed following the return of mass unemployment at the beginning of the 1980s. As a result, the official rate of unemployment ran at a figure 3 per cent lower. These changes are frequently explained in terms of UK governments' desire to 'massage' the unemployment statistics in order to head off public opposition to its economic policies, but Piore (1987) points out that changes in who counts as unemployed can be expected at times of crisis and that they are a sign of change in institutional structures.

In Chapter 1 I made the point that the real labour market was far too complex and ephemeral to present itself for counting and concluded that some sort of decision to *construct* it has to be made in any case. Maurice *et al.* (1986) conclude that when the labour market is going through a big change (with or without state help), changes in methods of counting will follow as part of the remaking, or reconstructing, that the state is attempting at this time of crisis.

Employment

The literature reviewed by Piore also demonstrates how employment comes to be the concern of the state, and so is constructed as a particular sort of employment, but we have already reviewed the basis of this argument in the previous subsection and there is no need to repeat it here. Instead, the present subsection is intended to illustrate in more detail the mechanisms by which polity values come to affect the labour market behaviour of workers and employers.

We begin by considering the translation of employment values into legislation (and policy) on *who* should be employed and *where* (we might have rehearsed these arguments for the unemployed too, of course). Through legislation, for example, the state decides who should be employed and who should not. It distinguishes categories of people who enter employment under special conditions (or not at all): older workers, different 'races' and ethnic groups, women, children, foreign nationals and people with a disability for example (Offe, 1985).

The creation of such special categories frequently involves the designation, by the state, of particular jobs as appropriate to particular workers. Such direction took place in a more general way in the United Kingdom during the Second World War and in South Africa for most of the post-war period (Cohen, 1987); and the direction of workers without citizenship rights has occurred in the United States (Piore, 1980) and in Western Europe (Böhning, 1972; Castles and Kosack, 1973). The freedom of labour to move from place to place has been created, sometimes facilitated, and often hindered by the state (Miles, 1990). As far as Britain is concerned, internal migration in the United Kingdom was once controlled by legislation (Hobsbawm, 1964; Redford, 1926); workers' freedom of movement within those countries which had made up the British Empire was first sanctioned and then abolished (Fryer, 1984; Rich, 1986); and freedom of movement within the European Community is now to be encouraged. Changes in the state's view on freedom of movement have, if anything, been even more important in the history of labour markets in the United States (Piore, 1987). Keyssar (1986), for example, contributes to a description of the 'casual labour market' that was created in the United States as a result of large-scale immigration, *and* to the description of the process whereby the proportion of more permanent employment increased when this immigration was halted.

The state's role in deciding where people can be employed is not, of course, simply a matter of controls on geographical movement. UK legislation prohibiting the employment of certain groups of workers on shift work or night work has been particularly significant in certain industries. Fevre (1984) describes changes in technology which produced a change in the hours of work in the wool textile industry and the subsequent replacement of women workers, who were disqualified from night work, by male immigrant workers. Ashton *et al.* (1990) explain the significance of legislation prohibiting the employment of youths on shift-work in preventing their employment in capital-intensive manufacturing firms. In the United Kingdom, there are further legislative restrictions on the employment of women down coal mines, while people with criminal records are disqualified from a number of jobs, and people without the proper qualifications are not allowed to practise medicine. In recent times, however, the state has legislated against the use of union membership as a proper qualification for employment (in a 'closed shop').

In France, the state is involved in a detailed system of job classification which assigns appropriate jobs to appropriate workers (Maurice *et al.*, 1986) that has no parallel in the United Kingdom, although the UK public employment service does tell people what vacancies are available and what vacancies are suitable for them. The public employment service also helps employers with screening, lay-offs and redundancies. In Sweden the public employment service does all these things but to much greater effect. Lane (1987) describes how, in the Soviet Union, some white-collar workers are not graded according to the 'market' or 'cultural' criteria common in the West, but according to 'political' or 'ideological' criteria (also see Kertesi and Sziráczki, 1988).

Finally, the influence of employment values on the behaviour of the state has led to the definition and sanction of particular forms of employment contract: from the enforcement of craft indentures and the legislative approval of the worst excesses of early industrial capitalism (Hobsbawm, 1964; Thompson, 1974; Corrigan, 1977), to modern definitions of legal contracts of employment (Cornfield, 1981; De Grazia, 1984). Subsidiary aspects of employment contracts such as equal opportunities and the European 'Social Charter' have already been discussed in this chapter, but we must mention legislation on maternity rights here. In the 1980s, increasing numbers of women in the United Kingdom exercised their new legal right to return to the same job after childbirth. In consequence, there was some change in the pattern described by Dex (1987 – see p. 56 above): proportionately fewer British women changed the industries in which they worked (and suffered downward social mobility as a result) when they returned to work after childbirth. According to McRae and Daniel (1991), growing numbers of women went back to the jobs they had left (and did so more quickly than before), and an increasing proportion of these women returned as full-timers rather than part-timers.

We might also mention the state's role in defining the circumstances under which contracts should end, and, therefore, the state's role in firing. In the United Kingdom the breach of a contract of employment by a worker was once considered a breach of criminal law whereas the employer's breach of contract was a civil offence. In the second half of the twentieth century, UK governments have placed a number of restrictions (some of them since rescinded) on employers' freedom to fire under the rubric of 'employment protection' legislation and procedures for short-time working, temporary lay-offs and redundancies.[5] French history tells how the state changed the nature of the employment contract by forcing industries to adopt the large enterprise model, for example by encouraging mergers between firms. The values of the large enterprise were then adopted by the business world (Salais *et al.*, 1986).

Education and training

The purpose of this final subsection is to give final confirmation of the effect of polity values on labour markets by showing how a variety of sociological perspectives concur on this point. More specifically, it will demonstrate that each of the three sociological theories of the state described earlier in this chapter leads to the common conclusion that the state facilitates the operation of labour markets through its control of education and training. Towards the end of this discussion it will, however, become clear that this simple conclusion is slightly misleading in that it gives no proper guide to the *sociological* contribution to our understanding of the subject. It is, after all, not the simple facts of education and training that are of most concern here, but education and training values, and it is through these values that (by way of the ministry of the state) labour markets are, in this instance, affected.

We begin with the view which we have identified, in its practical application, with corporatism: the idea that the state exists to further the aims of industrialism. In this view, the education and training system provided by the state should, for example, train people in the skills required to maintain economic development and growth. One of the main purposes of education, and the main purpose of training, is to make the supply side of the labour market fit the demand side. State education and training exists to produce appropriate numbers of workers with the right sort of characteristics (mostly defined in terms of possession of various sorts of 'skills') for the different sorts of jobs that have to be filled.

The existence of this relationship between education and training and labour markets is believed to explain why the state has become involved in both activities. As industrial development occurs the need for education and training increases (because, for example, there are more and bigger labour markets then more people are needed, and higher skills and a greater variety of skills are required) so the state takes on a role in education and training to achieve the aim of making supply fit demand. In support of this view, we can point to cases where the state has taken on such a role with the explicit aim of making supply fit demand. Such an aim is usually treated as axiomatic as far as training is concerned so we would be better advised to look at education.

The origins of free and compulsory public education in a variety of countries are most frequently explained in terms of the state's concern over the relationship between education and labour markets, for instance, as the product of the state's discovery that skills such as literacy and numeracy are required of the labour force in industrial societies. Maurice *et al.* (1986) also emphasise the contribution of education to the acquisition of 'tacit skills' (see p. 109 above, and Williams, 1974). The structure of public education systems is frequently explained in these terms too: the partition of such systems is believed to reflect the varying needs of employers (this much is often said of the UK 'tripartite' system of education, but also see Maurice *et al.*, 1986 on France and Germany; and Byrne, 1978; Deem, 1980 on the gender-partition of education).

Orthodox Marxist theorists might not dispute this analysis but would, rather, question why the state, and not workers' organisations, churches, or even employers, should play a leading role in the provision of education and training. In this view the state is not a neutral hand-maiden of industrialism and does not give, for example, the same weight to getting people into jobs (perhaps even ones they would like) – when providing education and training – that it does to finding labour for employers. What the employers want is much more important to the state than what the people want. The real consumers of (state) education and training are capitalists, not those who are educated and trained.

The state's involvement in education and training is therefore to be explained in terms of the state's role as an instrument of the capitalist class. Through education and training the state provides capitalists with the numbers and types of workers they need. It does so at reduced cost (paid for by workers through taxation), more efficiently (through economies of scale, and because the state need not worry about poaching), and (in many instances) on a compulsory basis.

Once this is said, the problem for Marxists becomes what might otherwise have been a minor issue: what about the workers who are not educated or trained? This is not a problem in the sense that it challenges the assumed link between education and training and labour markets. After all, there are (or were) unskilled jobs for those without education and training to do. Thus the partial failure of the state to educate or train supports the central assumption that the state is managing all of education and training in the interests of capital (see, for example, Bowles and Gintis, 1976; Willis, 1977).

In addition, a variety of Marxist theories (Althusser, 1971; Bowles and Gintis, 1976) conclude that a part of the state's brief from capital (which it follows in the provision of education and training) is the reproduction of labour power *per se* and, indeed, the reproduction of the attitudes which are required of a pliant proletariat. As we might expect, ostensibly similar points are made by Weberian theorists who point to the role of public education in fostering a belief in meritocracy and rational-legal-universal principles, but here we are more interested in another aspect of Weberian theory: its capacity to deal with evidence that the types of theory discussed above cannot cope with, namely evidence of the apparent inefficiency of education and training (for example in the United Kingdom, see Leadbeater and Lloyd, 1986). That state education and training is not always all that it could be is certainly suggested by evidence of higher wages for scarce skills and by evidence of labour shortages (let alone of unemployment) which can be supposed either to impair economic development or to damage the interests of capitalists.

It seems that (see, for example, Berg, 1971; Illich, 1971) in some established industrial societies, many people take very little from state education and training, while others get the wrong sort of education and training. Moreover, employers do not value what we might think they should in the state's curriculum and do not value any of the state's efforts to educate and train very much. It is possible that what employers really get out of the process is a supply of workers who are restricted (to the advantage of their employers) to the particular types of employment appropriate to 'students' and 'trainees' (also see Schervish, 1983 on the role of state licensing in creating ILMs in the United States). There is also the question of screening.

Employers require labels in order to hire and fire (see the discussion of matching on pp. 74–5 above), and if rational-legal-universal certification is required then the state should underwrite it, not simply through the licensing of particular qualifications but through the whole public education system. This is particularly obvious in Japan where Japanese companies have recruiting agreements with schools. Rosenbaum and Kariya (1989) describe how, in these schools, direct competition (in the labour market) for jobs has been translated into academic competition. It was noted above that it is usually treated as simply axiomatic that the state's role in *training* is entirely explicable in terms of the assumed simple relationship with labour markets, even if (as in the United Kingdom) it is also assumed that state training is merely a device to reduce the unemployment figures. But the history of state training can also be read as the story of the state's burgeoning role in certification rather than in the transmission of skills (even 'tacit' ones). In established industrial societies the history of state involvement in professional and technical training is long and detailed and includes examples of state provision of certification as well as licensing or underwriting certificates provided by others. In all of these societies the state has provided and/or underwritten certification in the medical, teaching and social-welfare professions; in clerical training and in training for manual workers (see, for example, Maurice *et al.*, 1986).

The distinction between 'real' education and training and public education and training (in the United States) is ably drawn by Berg (1971), who concludes that there is too much education for some and too little for others. He sees this as the consequence of 'purposeless credential consciousness' (Berg, 1971, p. 196) under which educational requirements are raised without assessment of need. But it would be a mistake to conclude that we have simply discovered evidence of the incompetence or mendacity of the state. It is certainly true that, even when the state apparently does have the relationship between education and training and labour markets in its sights, it often seems entirely incapable of doing anything about it. Many writers have noted the failed and abandoned attempts at coherent policy in the United Kingdom and the enormous variations in spending on, coverage of, and type of education and training in similar societies (and see Ashton, 1988a, 1988b on the differences between the United Kingdom and

Canada). But what such research suggests is not variations in competence between different states so much as the invalidity of the first assumption, the assumption that the simple relationship between education and training and labour markets is the direct concern of the state when it formulates policy. Many policies which seem to reflect this concern have actually come about for entirely different reasons such as a belief in the virtue of personal development or as a result of religious and wider moral concerns (Berg, 1971 also mentions the self-interest of academia). Indeed, some state education and training actually gets in the way of the simple relationship – after all, all off-the-job training and education reduces the size of the workforce.

The foregoing reminds us that this has really been a discussion about education and training *values* which have an independent life outside labour markets. A similar conclusion could be reached on the basis of the much-praised work of Maurice *et al.* (1986) on the inter-relations between state, education and training and labour markets in France and Germany (also see Lee, 1989 on the United Kingdom). Maurice *et al.* describe, for example, the process whereby French school-leavers with few or no qualifications are much more likely than their German counterparts to seek a job instead of seeking occupational training (1986, p. 34). Furthermore, French training seems to occur *after* a person has been chosen for a job (in order to make them capable of the job), whereas in Germany training occurs before the allocation of workers to jobs (Maurice *et al.*, 1986, p. 118).

Education and training values are brought (by the state, for example) to the labour market but they are not created there and there is not one education and training value (the facilitation of the labour market) but several. Polity brings these education and training values to the labour market, but does not, necessarily, bring 'real' education and training.

CONCLUSIONS

Since we will shortly conclude the whole book, what is said below amounts to a postscript rather than a systematic attempt to conclude this chapter. The first point to note is that, in a way, this has not been an equal partner to Chapters 3 or 4 because we could have discussed something other than polity, for example geography (see, for instance, Danson, 1982, 1986; Martin and Rowthorn, 1986; Massey and Meagan, 1982) with similar results. The general aim of this chapter was simply to demonstrate that society and economy analyses do not exhaust the types of analysis available to labour market sociology. Polity was chosen because labour market sociologists have, to date, shown a little more interest in polity than they have in geography (leading to some neglect, particularly in the sociology of migration: see Miles, 1990).

The second point concerns what was said at the beginning of the chapter about over-concentration on the state to the exclusion of other aspects of polity. We might conclude that, in comparison with the state, other aspects of polity remain in an underdeveloped condition because of the narrow social-policy or political interests of the writers (left and right) who have concerned themselves with the subject, but polity, nevertheless, remains the key to our understanding. Certainly, nothing that was said in general terms in this chapter about the state could not also apply to other aspects of polity, and it is to be hoped that these other aspects will receive more attention in the future.

For example, it is certainly possible for political values to intrude (for example, amongst employers, job-seekers and trade unions: compare the United Kingdom or France to Germany, see Maurice *et al.*, 1986; Windolf and Wood, 1988; see also Crompton and Sanderson, 1990) where the state does not (even as legislator). But in this case we should remember that these remain polity values. There is much research to be done but when it is, we must be sure it remains under the heading of polity.

To take an extreme example, it may be the politics of an employer that makes him or her keen on equal opportunities; and, in similar vein, we might consider the activities of the Economic League. This is a British organisation which provides details of job-seekers to the companies (some of which are known throughout the world) which subscribe to its service. In practice, the Economic League keeps a 'blacklist' of 'potential trouble-makers' with details of political affiliations and past political and trade union activity. Theory which does not refer to polity provides no *direct* explanation of why employers use the services of the Economic League as part of the informing process. Any adequate explanation must also refer, for example, to long-standing British concerns about 'politically-motivated strikes' and 'mindless militancy'.

NOTES

1. We should not, however, over-estimate the labour market effect of such policy changes in the United Kingdom which have, perhaps, been less important than had been hoped in some quarters. The increase in temporary workers has been largely confined to employment in education, and where casualisation has occurred it has usually been as a consequence of privatisation (Ascher, 1987; Fevre, 1991; Pollert, 1987). Readers might like to note an extreme example of the importance of ideology provided by reforming Hungary where the demand for labour exceeded the supply of labour. Here firms used ideological arguments to persuade the state to allow them to compete for scarce labour, for example by offering higher wages (Kertesi and Sziráczki, 1988, p. 307).
2. This even applies in the case of 'corporatist' employers and trade unions, for example in Germany. When employers and trade unions act with national unemployment, employment, or education and training in mind, they are being influenced by polity values (and usually must act in concert with the state, of course). Also see Offe (1985).
3. For all three the problem of relevance arises once more. Here we are primarily interested in things that are directly relevant to labour markets – things (structures, relationships and so on) that have a direct effect on the workings of labour markets. Of course, when it comes to real cases the judgement of direct or indirect is usually a matter of judging degree, but the key point is that we should try to keep down the number of references to polity influences that are only relevant to labour markets at several removes because to have any effect they must be mediated by any number of other things discussed in earlier chapters. For example, in the sub-section on employment, legislation on redundancy procedures will be considered directly relevant to the sociology of labour markets whereas legislation concerning health and safety at work will not.
4. The view taken by MacInnes (1987) recalls that of Keane and Owens with the crucial difference that MacInnes sees this as a reversible

process whereas Keane and Owens are not at all sure that full employment can be achieved again. MacInnes, indeed, thinks that the full-employment welfare state can be rebuilt on stronger foundations (if only both sides of industry would abandon their commitment to 'voluntarism').

5. The severity of these restrictions may of course vary according to the category of employment, decided by industry, by size, by legal ownership category (for example, 'self-employed'), by markets (for example, export), by location (for example, 'enterprise zone' in the United Kingdom, see also Offe, 1985), and so on.

6

THEORY AND METHOD

According to Michael Rose, 'sociologists have never managed to systematize their observations about the operation of labour markets' (Rose, 1988, P. 325). This book has attempted to fill the gap that Rose identifies, and so this concluding chapter has two aims: to summarise what really matters in the sociological contribution to the study of labour markets; and to describe, in outline, what seem to be the most likely future developments in the field. If both of these aims can be achieved we will be in a position to see what sociology can contribute to the future interdisciplinary study of labour markets. Although Rose's comment was a response to sociologists' distrust of the 'schematic' nature of some labour market economics, an interest in the future prospects for interdisciplinary study probably lies behind Rose's terse criticism. It is certainly easy to see that sociology cannot contribute what it might to interdisciplinary study if it is not systematised. In other words, how can we expect a discipline to contribute if we do not know what the *contribution* is? Similarly, the effort to systematise the sociology of labour markets should also bring dividends for sociology since the subject area might someday be in a position to pay back what it owes to the discipline. It will be argued that, in both cases, the most important contribution of labour market sociology turns out to be something we might not have expected: its *method*.

Towards the end of this chapter I will describe what I see as the basic outline of the method of the sociology of labour markets, but this would make little sense if I did not first describe how we have reached this point. We have reached it through a process (spanning five chapters) which began with the definition of the

subject matter, leading to a search for appropriate and useful
theory, and ending in the construction of (in fact, to some extent,
the borrowing of – see below) a method by which we might apply
the theory to the subject matter.[1]

Thus, in Chapter 1, we began the attempt to systematise
sociological work on labour markets by constructing a definition
of our subject matter in the abstract. By (mis)using Thomas Hardy
we were able to construct a five-process model of the labour
market, but we were immediately confronted by a variety of
problems which arose when we tried to put this abstract definition
into practice. Most obviously, we were confronted with the
problem that our abstract model made no reference to the labour
market territories that we encountered in the real world of
modern labour markets.

The remaining chapters investigated the relationship between
the abstract model and the complex reality of modern labour
markets. Each chapter was intended to address the problem of
how the abstract becomes (or does not become) concrete by way
of sociological explanation. In the first instance, we were required
to find a theory, or, rather, to find the many theories which we
would need if we were to understand the diversity and complexity
of modern labour markets.

THE THEORY OF THE SOCIOLOGY OF LABOUR MARKETS

In Chapter 3 we began to look at sociologists' explanations of the
origin and nature of labour markets. These explanations amounted
to the two social principles of the social division of labour and
social hierarchy.

The theories of the social division of labour which we
considered were agreed that increasing differentiation between
people and between work occurred with social development. Some
variants suggested that this differentiation occurred on the basis of
'natural' differentiation and the obvious advantages of specialisation, and they offered some explanation of rudimentary informing, screening and offering processes, but these suggestions were
not wholly persuasive and begged the question of values. They did
not concern themselves with the processes whereby the things

people do, and the people themselves, are evaluated according to general criteria.

Theories which referred to values were discussed in relation to the second social principle of social hierarchy on which the social division of labour actually depends. Without the principle of hierarchy there can be no development of the social division of labour. The social division of labour calls for rudimentary labour market processes because if we do not all do the same thing we have a problem of distributing people to labours and labours to people, but there is no way of distributing people or things to do without values. There would be no social division of labour – the question simply would not arise – without the principle of hierarchy: qualitative differences between labours and between people. Labour market processes are therefore established, and their fundamental nature decided, by the social division of labour *and* by hierarchical solutions to problems of distributing people and work in this division of labour.

In Chapter 3 we were concerned with the social division of labour in which not everyone does the same thing (work) and different people become responsible for different things to do. In Chapter 4 we found that labour markets require the exchange of labour power which then produces the economic division of labour, that is the division of labour between jobs (places for which labour is bought and sold) and workers (categories of labour which are bought and sold). Chapter 4 therefore raised the problem of distributing workers to jobs and not simply people to work. It made our explanations a great deal more comprehensive in consequence since we were no longer concerned with rudimentary labour market processes, but with proper labour markets (whose existence and development is of course contingent on the development of exchange). Nevertheless, the new problem (of distributing workers to jobs) would not be raised, let alone solved, without the second social principle already discussed in Chapter 3: the principle of social hierarchy which allows values to be attached to workers and jobs.

We discussed three versions of explanations of the basis of social hierarchy. Firstly, we discussed hierarchy based on people values in which workers and jobs are assigned values according to general criteria derived from the supposed existence of a hierarchy of people categories. People are the source of the hierarchical principle and workers are judged according to who they are, and the job according to whose job it is.

Secondly, we discussed hierarchy based on work values in which jobs and workers are assigned values according to general criteria derived from a supposed hierarchy of jobs, for example a hierarchy based on the usefulness (to society) of various jobs. People are judged according to what job they do, or are capable of doing. The five labour market processes then distribute different jobs to the appropriate (capable) workers.

Finally, we looked at market values as a basis for hierarchy. Here we attended to relations between jobs and workers as the source of values. These relations created both the hierarchies (of jobs and of workers) and solved the distribution problem: the market situation of workers and jobs tells us the relationship of one worker to another and one job to another *and* decides which worker gets which job. This was not a question of fitting the best people to the best jobs, but of fitting one to the other in a legitimate way. The market is believed to be a way of bringing about a perfect distribution method, or a good approximation of it.

The five labour market processes are the concrete expression of this legitimating process: they decide the market situation of the person and work and distribute accordingly. The determination of market situation can involve all of the things discussed in other theories (gender of person/job, capability of person/function of job) but these are now to be seen as signs. But there is, nevertheless, a tendency to particular sorts of signs – rational-legal-universal signs – as time goes by, since it is the increased acceptance of rational-legal-universal principles that in any case explains why the market itself (including the labour market) should be accepted as a legitimate distribution mechanism.

We then turned (in Chapter 3) to the day-to-day workings of labour markets, the social interaction through which the five labour market processes are actually experienced. Chapter 3 gave us three theories of this interaction. The terms 'discrimination', 'selection' and 'matching' described the social processes which occurred when people values, work values and market values, respectively, determined the operation of labour markets.

There would be no discrimination, selection or matching if it were not for the existence of social groups, relations and institutions. The sections on social groups, relations and institutions in Chapters 3 and 4 showed how the idea of values (of any kind) being relevant to the problem of distributing workers to jobs (or jobs to workers) comes into being with groups, relations and institutions, and how it works through these same groups, relations and institutions.

In Chapter 3 the relevant sub-section described a variety of explanations of the way in which the two social principles of division of labour and hierarchy were put into practice. These explanations – which referred to the key sociological concepts of 'culture' and 'power' – included status attainment theory and its variants, and theories of social closure and domination.

In Chapter 4 the equivalent sub-section described three ways of looking at the effects of the economic division of labour: in terms of specialisation and cooperation, exploitation and conflict, and legitimacy and the market. The difference between these explanations lay precisely in differences of opinion about what (important) social groups, relations and institutions are created in the economic division of labour. In the second half of Chapter 4 it was demonstrated, nevertheless, that each of these theories could be understood to agree (albeit in very different ways) on the contribution of economic, technical and organisational values – collectively termed industrial values – to our understanding of labour markets. Labour markets may always be social processes but they will nevertheless be informed (are always informed in established industrial societies) by industrial values too.

In Chapter 5 we intended to look at the contribution of polity studies to labour market sociology. Polity has an influence on labour markets through political organisations like the state acting as an employer and through political government. Polity brings with it formal authority: this means new groups, relations, and institutions to consider in the shape of political parties, lobbies, government and so on. But because so much attention had been paid to the state in the relevant literature, there was no discussion of 'social groups, relations and institutions' in this chapter, but only a sub-section on three sociological theories of the state which arise from different views of what the state is about. Nevertheless (and just as in Chapter 4), these different theories concurred on the influence of the state on labour markets as a bearer of polity values. Thus labour market processes, while always social, can be influenced by polity values as well as industrial values. The examples of polity values given in Chapter 5 were, of course, unemployment, employment, and education and training.

THE METHOD OF THE SOCIOLOGY OF LABOUR MARKETS

In Chapter 3 we considered the dangers of conceptual inflation in respect of discrimination, selection and matching. If these concepts were made to mean too much they became useless to us, and the search for a 'grand theory' which could tell us everything we needed to know about labour markets was, we concluded, futile (at least as far as the sociology of labour markets was concerned). This conclusion was held as axiomatic in later chapters – grand theory was to be avoided whenever we encountered a new theory or idea – but we did not deal, at any length, with the central problem which arises when we do *not* conceptually inflate.

If we have a variety of theories, none of which is meant to explain everything, how do we ever choose between them? The answer that has been given throughout is that we decide which theory applies in any particular (concrete) case *on empirical grounds*. Now, while this is essentially correct, it is not (yet) saying much. What does 'deciding which theory is correct on empirical grounds' really mean; where do we start? We start with the accounts of what goes on in labour markets which are offered by the people involved in them, workers and employers for example.

We start with lay explanations of what goes on in labour markets because, once we have eliminated the possibility of the existence of general laws for social interaction – and this possibility is eliminated along with grand theory – we are left with what displaced them (see pp. 79–81 above): the idea of the social construction of social phenomena. So, we, as sociologists, are interested in labour markets as social constructions. Making and explaining are closely related activities in social construction, so somewhere in the lay explanations we will find what we want to know. Let me explain this in a little more detail.

In a social construction like the labour market, the process whereby people explain what is going on, and the process whereby they create the thing, or make things go on, are closely related. For example, peoples' views of how labour markets work (or should work) can help to make labour markets what they are. The same point can apply when academic theories become lay theories, that is when the explaining of academics is related to the making of labour markets, for example when the state makes use of a sociologist's theory. On occasion academic theories become part of the phenomena we study and in Chapters 1 and 5 we encountered cases of the state explicitly constructing labour markets in a particular way. For instance, in Chapter 1 we referred to UK governments' attempts to make labour markets work in the way that they were supposed to according to (some) economists' theories. In Chapter 5 we noted the connection between sociological theory and the practice of corporatism. These examples say nothing about the value (or otherwise) of social scientific theory as a guide to policy. They are only mentioned here to illustrate the fact that explaining and making activities can become very closely related. If this can happen in the case of academic theory, it is even more likely to happen as far as lay theories are concerned.

Chapter 5 also included a brief discussion of (changes in) official methods of counting the numbers of unemployed. This discussion illustrates the close relationship between explanation and creation in social construction. Counting is often (although most obviously when done by the state) a way of making as well as explaining. UK governments made thirty changes in the way the unemployed were counted in the 1980s with the declared aim of making the official statistics a better representation of the true picture. Yet each change altered the picture that was being represented, not least by affecting the behaviour of the unemployed themselves, especially those who were no longer officially counted as unemployed. Official statistics are an illustration of the social construction of unemployment and so statistics are a resource for other reasons than what we learn from the statistical details: what is compiled and how it is compiled help us to find out what is going on. Government statistical methods become a useful object of our study rather than an aid to it.

Readers who are sociologists will recognise something of the work of Cicourel (1968) on juvenile crime in the foregoing. The method of the sociology of labour markets borrows ideas from a variety of different places (including systems theory, for example – see Hodgson, 1988; the work of Bourdieu – see Maurice *et al.*, 1986, pp. 231–4 and Piore, 1987; and perhaps even the Marxist method of 'praxis'), but the view of method given here owes much to interactionist, and even ethnomethodological treatments. Throughout the book there have been attempts to ground explanations in social interaction, like hiring and firing, in the way that interpretative sociology suggests we should. This has been done in order to fill the space between 'structure' and 'action' which we encounter in some sociological methods, and so to avoid creating further difficulties such as the problem of 'agency' (Giddens, 1984).

Now this is all very well; the method of the sociology of labour markets has good sociological credentials, but what does it do? According to the argument so far, lay explanation of what goes on in labour markets is a resource for sociologists because each lay explanation, each interpretation, is potentially a description of how the thing was made to happen. The opinions of each lay person may give us a vital clue in our search for the appropriate sociological theory. But which opinion is the right one in any particular situation, which one gives us the 'real' evidence? We seem only to have re-stated our initial problem: instead of wondering how we choose between different academic theories, we now puzzle over the choice between different lay interpretations. Different lay perceptions are an essential resource, perhaps, but they don't agree!

The empirical evidence will rarely, if ever, lend unambiguous support to one theory or another. The ambiguous nature of evidence derives from the availability of alternative interpretations of what is going on – not the alternative theories propounded by sociologists but the alternative interpretations offered by lay people. Consider, for example, the difficulties faced by a researcher who investigates a case of mass redundancy. The researcher may well find that the redundancies are interpreted in one way by managers, in another by trade union officials, and in a variety of different ways by the redundants themselves and the workers who remain in employment.

Readers will remember the (mock) dismay with which theory competition was greeted: having more than one theory to choose from seemed to produce an impossible situation. For example, in the worst case different theories did not simply disagree on the interpretation of the same evidence, but even on what was to be explained. We then discovered that this was not a problem at all, but a resource. We needed a portfolio of different theories because labour markets were so complex and difficult to explain. The same might be said of lay theories too, of course, but, on the other hand, how *do* we find out which explanation is the one that really matters?

We have established that modern labour markets are complex and difficult to explain because they are social constructions; and it should be no surprise that a social construction will give rise to equally complex and diverse social interpretation of what is going on (by the people involved, for example). Since the labour market is a social construction we would expect there to be more than one lay view of how the labour market works,[2] for example, but how can we decide which explanation matters? First of all, we need to work out what we really mean by 'the explanation that matters'. We find that there are at least three types of explanation which we might encounter in empirical research: accounts of what happened/happens *and* rationalisations and accounts of intentions.

Personnel managers who recruit people and successful applicants for vacancies are quite likely to tell researchers (or anyone else who asks them) that the process of hiring that they have been engaged in was a process of selection in which the best applicant was chosen for the job. They will tend to say this even if the hiring process was discriminatory because there is generally more cultural – for example, moral – acceptance of selection in established industrial societies.

Job-seekers will seek to explain what happens in the labour market in the way that suits them. If you are a successful applicant for a job you are more likely to think you got it by a process of selection because you approve of this way of running labour markets, and know that others approve too. It makes you feel good to think you got the job because you were the most capable applicant (judged according to the apparently impersonal and objective criteria of what the job entailed, which were derived from the work itself).

The same is true of those who do the recruiting. No matter what the actual facts of the case are, a personnel manager will be inclined to tell you that he or she *selects* the best people for the jobs on offer, that he or she hires and fires according to work values. If personnel managers cannot always say that they selected in the way they wanted to, for example if they are offering lower wages than they would ideally like, and believe that the workers they hire are less capable as a result, then they simply say they are selecting the best workers that they can under the circumstances. They are unlikely to say, even in such extreme cases, that the labour market is matching workers to jobs. For one thing, this observation makes the recruiting function of personnel management seem an unnecessary expense which employers can well do without.

Readers might also like to note that the propensity of all recruiters to explain their activities in terms of selection makes hiring appear as a process of inclusion and not exclusion (cf. Offe, 1985). Any exclusion which occurs is simply an unfortunate side-effect of the hiring process, and this explains the conundrum which is frequently encountered in labour market sociology: groups of workers – perhaps black workers, young workers or women – who are thought to be excluded groups are included (and given jobs) when there are no alternative workers available. This is explained by what is said by the personnel manager who *has* employed black workers, young workers or women. The personnel manager will say, as ever, that hiring was a process of selection. The researcher who hears this concludes that the workers in question were included, but makes a mistake if they think they have come across an unusual recruiter. If there is always talk of inclusion after the fact (of hiring) we will only hear such talk in relation to excluded groups where they *are* included, but exactly the same thing could be said of any other group of workers in the labour market. In all of these cases we are documenting the rationalisations that occur after the fact.

Failed applicants who say that there was discrimination in the recruitment process are alleging that they were excluded (and that any inclusion would have been a fortunate by-product). If you do not get a job you are more likely to think that people-based values (and perhaps even market values) were used in recruitment.[3] You may well describe the hiring process using pejorative terms like 'discrimination' and 'favouritism' to convey that the process was unfair, that it was cheating.[4] You may even have a certain view of why people-based values were used. Perhaps you suffered discrimination because of social closure, or male domination? In any event, you are engaged in rationalising the outcome of the recruitment process.

When rationalising some example of social interaction, we are attempting to put our role in this interaction in the best possible light. A personnel manager who is in charge of recruitment will want to make his or her role in the interaction seem blameless in the same way that failed applicants want to see themselves in the right. But what makes the process of rationalisation especially complex, and therefore even more interesting to us, is that one of the ways in which we seek to rationalise our roles – to make them seem good to others – is to, firstly, describe our roles as active ones, and, secondly, to describe the actions that we took in these roles as intentional. Thus the personnel manager who is responsible for hiring will not tell the researcher that he or she took no active part in recruitment and nor will he or she say that they did not 'know what they were doing'. Instead, personnel managers usually tell researchers that they have policies which are designed to permit the selection of workers and that they take actions which are intended to put these policies into effect, and which actions have the desired (and intended) result.

Not only are rationalisations after the fact unreliable descriptions of social interaction, but so are descriptions of intentions. Evidence of intentions is unreliable precisely because intentional action is what is expected, is what is supposed to be a good thing. Furthermore, intentions are not the only causes of action and still less are they the dominant factors on every occasion. Existing practices and rules, for example, can be far more important when we consider what factors have informed a particular action (see for example, the discussion of custom in recruitment practices in Windolf and Wood, 1988; see also Hodgson, 1988; Marsden, 1986). Let us refer to the earlier discussion of inclusion and exclusion in order to illustrate this point.

A recruiter might intend to keep black workers in particular sorts of jobs (for example, the worst jobs) but this intention is only indirectly related to the actions that actually put blacks in the worst jobs.[5] People, work or market values are terms which describe the criteria according to which a personnel manager decides whether to accept or reject a candidate. These criteria may very well be unrelated to personnel managers' intentions which *appear* to embody one or other of these type of criteria.[6] Thus a recruiter may be a racist or may want to keep women in the home but, when hiring, the recruiter may use a different set of people values entirely to effect a decision. For example, perhaps his or her company requires the recruitment of younger workers for positions as trainees. A (not so hypothetical) demographic imbalance in the local supply of labour means that the vast majority of applicants for these positions are black, whereas older applicants for vacancies tend to be white. Despite his or her intentions, therefore, the recruiter ends up hiring (young) black workers.

Similarly, a personnel manager who intends to use people values in hiring and firing may even use a different value base altogether and may not discriminate at all. Thus the personnel manager who is instructed to make voluntary redundancies might intend to use this device to reduce the percentage of women in the workforce, but finds that voluntary redundancy is a matching process in which, on this occasion, more men than women volunteer. This may happen because, for example, male employees have longer service and so are entitled to larger severance payments, or have better prospects (than women) of finding alternative jobs.

Readers will see that the reverse of this case is also possible. A recruiter's intentions may be anti-racist yet their actions take the form of racial discrimination. Such a recruiter will intend to avoid the use of people values in recruitment because they deplore the exclusion of black workers from some jobs. They intend, therefore, to use work or market values in recruitment, but fear that selection or matching will not produce enough successful black candidates. They therefore give extra weight to the candidacies of black applicants and thereby introduce a people value into the recruitment process.

Something similar might be said of job-seekers. They may intend to exclude jobs that they do not approve of (divorce attorney) and to include jobs that they respect (nurse), but a great many other things must happen before they can avoid being divorce lawyers and manage to become nurses. For instance, they may have other intentions, like the intention to earn a lot of money, which conflict with their intentions to include or exclude particular jobs. Similarly, consider the feminist who is determined that she should have a career which gives the lie to the stereotype of a woman who works only for 'pin-money', and who, in search of that career, joins a profession (teacher, social worker) which is popularly considered feminine. To some degree, she has confirmed what she intended to deny, namely that women workers are not interchangeable with men.

Accounts of intentions are unreliable because intentions are often constructed in retrospect, and intentions are in any case frequently unconsummated. They are unconsummated because a person's intentions conflict with each other, or conflict with other peoples' intentions, or because any intentions they have are unrelated to their actions (also see Weber, 1964, 1968). Thus, so far as our present purposes are concerned, we require a method of filtering out the accounts of rationalisations or intentions from lay explanations since these are unreliable as evidence of what really happened, or what is really going on. We have solved this problem in practice many times in the foregoing chapters, but now we need to know the procedure, in other words the method of the sociology of labour markets must be made explicit. We need to know the method in order to decide whether it is a good method and, especially, so that we can find ways of improving it.

Our problem is alternative evidences which derive from alternative lay understandings. These alternatives exist because there are at least three categories of understanding and our task is to decide which explanations refer to rationalisations, which to intentions and which remain. The method of the sociology of labour markets can be termed 'deconstruction':[7] in each enquiry into labour markets that we undertake, we must deconstruct the process by which our case became the way it is. At the end of our deconstruction we will have explained the case, not only how it happened, but also what is going on now. For example, we will be able to say whether there is evidence of discrimination, selection, or matching, or some combination of these processes.

Why is the method deconstruction? The answer to this question is implicit in what has been said in this chapter so far, but I will put it in another way. Without it our sociology of labour markets is merely a (sophisticated) way of *documenting* how labour markets work, for example we find an 'internal labour market' in a firm or an industry. Ideally we also need a method for explaining how this came about. We may discover – on empirical grounds – that employers are in command in one industry and not another. We can then continue the analysis to find out how this situation came about, how it was made, and not simply how it works. How did these particular employers get into the position of having (or not having) power? Instead of simply saying 'things are different in different labour markets' – or, in more academic terms, referring to the 'historical specificity of concrete cases' – we can seek some sociological explanation in the fullest sense of the term. If we are to do more than simply document (the sociological aspects of) labour markets, if we are, rather, to explain what has happened and what is going on, we must demonstrate how our choices between theories, which we make on empirical grounds, come to be valid in any substantive case. This really means only that we must find out how the empirical grounds came to be what they are, and this activity is synonymous with deconstruction.

It is this method that puts us in the position to do more than simply document labour markets: to do sociology and explain why labour markets differ, for instance why a particular labour market presents the mix of evidence (a bit of discrimination, some influence from technical values and so on) that we can explain with a particular set of theories. We will now describe and (simultaneously) exemplify the deconstruction method. In very simple terms, this method suggests that we should always work through the stages described above in respect of the *whole* of the sociology of labour markets every time we wish to understand a specific case.

An outline of method

The whole book has in fact been a description of method, but there follows a short summary of the resulting guidelines which are used in any particular case (although this is rarely made explicit, however Maurice *et al.* 1986, for example, attempt something similar in their appendix). In the first instance, we must discover, on the basis of empirical research, whether our case should be understood in terms of analysis at the level of society, economy, polity, or perhaps even geography (this is not an exhaustive list) or some combination of these. We are then able to decide which theories are, in principle, relevant to our case. Although we may be able, for example, to rule out polity straight away (for instance, if the actions of state have no direct influence on our case), it is unlikely that we will want to rule out too many theories at this stage.

At the next stage we must establish what social groups, relations and institutions are relevant, again on the basis of empirical evidence. For example, are the workers involved also professionals, are they members of trade unions, is there evidence that the designation of people by 'race' or gender is relevant to our case? But the field from which we draw our explanations will not be appreciably narrowed until we reach the third stage of our process of deconstruction.

It is in the third stage that we seek to filter out rationalisations and accounts of intentions and so to establish which accounts are not merely explanations of our case but constructions of it (they are 'makings' as well as 'explainings' – see p. 156 above). In large part, we do this by investigating questions of power and culture. In the most simple terms, a social group may be able to make their account matter because they have the power to do so (also see Offe, 1985).

It is the researcher's task to establish whether this is indeed the case: can the group in question compel others to go along? Consider, for example, the role of some trade unions in determining the employment patterns of black workers in the United Kingdom. One common account has it that the unions act to exclude black workers from better jobs. Research may certainly establish that such exclusion is intended, but is this why black workers are under-represented in better jobs? To answer this question research must establish whether or not trade unions have the power to exclude black workers in this way, and we may then conclude that the unions' intentions are irrelevant. For example (see Fevre, 1985), if real power rests with the employers, and employers will only recruit black workers where white workers are not available (that is, in the worst jobs), then trade unions play no active role in determining the employment distribution of black workers.

Research should not, however, concern itself with questions of power alone. For example, if it is not to use physical force, a social group may have to possess culturally sanctioned power to play an active role. Indeed, cultural sanction of power may not be adequate without a cultural mechanism by which one group's account can become *the* construction of the labour market. Power may have to be supplemented by sanction (for the construction) from the common culture to which all the social groups involved belong. It is for this reason that researchers attend to questions of custom and practice, and tradition, in their investigations.

For example, we saw in Chapter 3 that job-seekers have different orientations – some prefer outdoor work for example – but we need to ask whether such orientations are culturally-sanctioned as important influences on the labour market. It may be that job-seekers would like to choose jobs which they find interesting but Blackburn and Mann (1979) report that there is no mechanism by which these likes and dislikes can have much effect on the way labour markets work.

In practice, research will rarely be concerned with simple questions of power or culture but rather with complicated questions of power and culture. Let us say working class families bring their children up to believe in work as *the* source of value (and that manual work is more useful than non-manual work). Now, there may cultural sanction for this belief, but does this result in higher pay for manual work? Can members of the working class change those bits of the labour market which are run with people or the market as the source of value? Can they even maintain jobs as the source of value in those parts of the labour market where this is presently the case? Cultural sanction may not amount to much unless it is combined with power. For example, a family may be able to stop you marrying out of a social group (or into one) but will be less likely to be able to do something about your labour market experience, unless it also has economic power (the family owns a firm, or is a trade union dynasty) or political power.

At the end of the complicated third stage of research, we are in a position to reach a series of conclusions about the *operative* values in our case. To return to an earlier, simple example, trade unions may well think that the labour market is about jobs for whites and act as if the labour market could distribute in this way. They may even try to make it work like this, but their (people) values are not the operative values for labour markets because there is no mechanism to make them operational. By process of elimination we are able to conclude which values matter, that is, we can discover the values according to which the labour market is constructed. When we discover the operative values for the social processes of hiring and firing we will be able to conclude whether this is a process of selection, discrimination or matching (or some combination of these three). We can then repeat the exercise for industrial values, polity values, and so on, in order to discover what other sorts of operative values have informed the construction of the labour market in the case in question.

Ideally, this exercise – the identification of operative social, industrial and polity values – should be repeated for each of the five labour market processes described in Chapter 1. For example, it is quite possible that the screening processes in a particular case of recruitment (or of separation from employment) amount to matching, whereas the offer of employment is an act of discrimination. While investigating each labour market process in turn, we may even discover why (see Chapter 1) some of these processes are truncated, extended or even collapsed. Thus a screening process may be perfunctory because it amounts to matching whereas discrimination is the dominant social process in the case which is being investigated.

Since this complicated method should be followed in every case we investigate, it is obvious that sociological research into labour markets is a slow and painstaking business, a matter of successive processes of elimination to be patiently exhausted rather than of insight born of genius. But what other method would we recommend researchers to follow when the aim is to explain complex reality?

CONCLUSION

The complexity of social phenomena requires a huge research effort to reach a reliable conclusion about the smallest and most confined example. Fortunately, the researcher can often find a short-cut to some conclusions by way of the established literature which reports the conclusions reached by other researchers who have investigated similar cases. Nevertheless, such research (and sociological research in general) is sometimes popularly seen as representing a huge expenditure of effort in order to say very little at the end of the process, in order, even, to state the obvious. This popular view is based on a misunderstanding. To the extent that it investigates phenomena (like labour markets) which are socially constructed, sociological research must reach a conclusion which will resonate with at least one lay interpretation. If it does *not* do this something is wrong. The difference between sociological research and popular opinion lies in the fact that the lay interpretation which resonates with the sociological conclusion remains one amongst many whereas, by virtue of slow and methodical research, the sociologist has established that, in their case, this interpretation is the one that really matters.

The foregoing summarises the contribution of sociology to the interdisciplinary study of labour markets that was mentioned at the beginning of this chapter. The contribution is not perhaps as glamorous as we might have hoped since it depends on painstaking research in case after case. Certainly we do not have to research every small part of the labour market in order to say something meaningful about the labour market in the United States or the United Kingdom since we can draw our conclusions on the basis of a sample, but we are still involved in laborious (and expensive) research in the cases which constitute our sample. This point is well-illustrated by the enormous research effort required in the United Kingdom to meet the aims of the Economic and Social Research Council's Social and Economic Life Initiative (see p. 20 above), and by the extraordinary rigour employed in American quantitative research within the sociology of labour markets (see, for example, Kaufman, 1986). There is, however, one aspect of the sociological contribution to interdisciplinary study that promises a little more excitement to researchers who long for flights of fancy rather than disciplined 'legwork'.

Chapter 4 alluded to this less prosaic aspect when economic values were introduced, and when it was stated that these were the province of economics, but before we follow up this allusion, we must first make clear that nothing that will be said below should be thought to undermine the value of economists' contributions to interdisciplinary study.[8] Chapter 1 established that economics and sociology are interested in labour markets for different reasons. Economists are interested in mechanisms for the distribution of resources; sociologists in how people end up in good and bad jobs. Furthermore, in Chapter 2 it was established that sociology and economics did not really share the same subject matter. It should not, therefore, be thought that there are valid grounds for competition between economics and sociology.

Readers should now be in no doubt that economics is indispensable to the interdisciplinary study of labour markets, but might not sociologists have something to say about why economics is so indispensable? If sociologists are prepared to treat social values, or polity values, in the way that they do – as something to be questioned and not to be taken for granted, as fodder for study – then why not treat economic values in the same way? Thus sociologists would investigate, using the key ideas of power and culture, the contribution of social groups, relations and institutions to economic values.

Weber comes close to doing this at times, and Marx referred to political economy as the 'bourgeois science'. More recently, the social anthropologist, Davis, has described the view of the market propounded by neo-classical economics as the moral goal of one section of society (Davis, 1985). Some economists (for example, Hodgson, 1988 and the literature he reviews) appear to be thinking along similar lines. Is it time for sociologists to ask who constructs labour markets in terms of economic values and when and where such constructions matter? The sociology of labour markets, along with the rest of economic sociology, may well find out that, in the end, it is the sociology of economics that pays back the debt that is owed to the discipline of sociology.

NOTES

1. This is a 'positivist' approach to the extent that I have believed the subject area necessarily 'brings with it' a theory and a method which is 'waiting to be discovered' and there may, of course, be limitations to such an approach.
2. And even – just as for academics – differences of opinion as to what the labour market is. For example, when I look for a job 'the labour market' will mean (to me) the available vacancies, perhaps even the vacancies for a particular job, vacancies for personnel officers for

example. If I get the job and end up recruiting people as part of my personnel duties, 'the labour market' becomes something altogether different: the volume and character of labour seeking employment in the sort of work I have to offer.

3. Similarly, personnel managers may claim that they use work-based values, but if they have to explain why a certain person in their employ is not very good at the job they may well say people-based values were used (by their predecessor!).

4. Note that if you thought there was no discrimination at all – for example if you saw the process as one of 'positive discrimination' – you would think it was not based on people values (colour was a qualification) or that this is a necessary corrective ('affirmative' action) to make the market work according to job-based values.

5. It makes no difference to this argument that intentions are not simply exclusive, for example we can introduce a rank order of more or less included jobs. There can even be an intention to absolutely exclude certain groups, but in this case a lot of other things have to happen before managers actually leave positions vacant, change the nature of the problematic jobs, or close down their firms.

6. Intentions are of course informed by views of social hierarchy. Both intentions and rationalisations are socially constructed, for example arise from identification with a particular social group.

7. Some readers may feel that the method described here also owes something to the 'archaeological method' employed by Foucault, 1970.

8. As exemplified, for example, by recent progress in the study of the 'circulation of labour power' (Purdy, 1988); and in the 'new' theories reviewed by Fallon and Verry (1988): 'job search theories' (for further review of the interdisciplinary use of the 'information goods approach' see Maurice *et al.*, 1986), 'contract theory', 'efficiency wage theory' and 'bargaining theory'.

BIBLIOGRAPHY

Albrow, M. (1970) *Bureaucracy*, London: Macmillan.

Althauser, R.P. and Kalleberg, A.L. (1981) 'Firms, occupations, and the structure of labour markets: a conceptual analysis', in I. Berg (ed.) *Sociological Perspectives on Labor Markets*, New York: Academic Press.

Althusser, L. (1971) 'Notes on ideology and ideological state apparatuses', in L. Althusser, *Lenin and Philosophy and Other Essays*, London: New Left Books, pp. 123-73.

Aries, P. (1973) *Centuries of Childhood*, Harmondsworth: Penguin.

Ascher, K. (1987) *The Politics of Privatisation: contracting out the public services*, London: Macmillan.

Ashton, D. (1986) *Unemployment Under Capitalism: the sociology of British and American labour markets*, Brighton: Wheatsheaf.

Ashton, D. (1988a) 'Educational institutions, youth and the labour market', in D. Gallie (ed.) *Employment in Britain*, Oxford: Basil Blackwell.

Ashton, D. (1988b) 'Sources of variation in labour market segmentation: a comparison of youth labour markets in Canada and Britain', *Work, Employment and Society*, vol. 2, no. 1, pp. 1–24.

Ashton, D., Maguire, M. and Spilsbury, M. (1990) *Restructuring the Labour Market; the implications for youth*, Basingstoke: Macmillan.

Atkinson, J. (1984) *Emerging UK Work Patterns*, Brighton: Institute for Manpower Studies.

Bacon, R. and Eltis, W. (1976) *Britain's Economic Problem: too few producers*, London: Macmillan.

Banton, M. (1983a) *Racial and Ethnic Competition*, Cambridge: Cambridge University Press.

Banton, M. (1983b) 'Categorical and statistical discrimination', *Ethnic and Racial Studies*, vol. 6, no. 4, pp. 269–83.

171

Banton, M. (1985) 'Name and substance: a response to criticism', *Ethnic and Racial Studies*, vol. 8, no. 4, pp. 590–5.

Barber, A. (1985) 'Ethnic origin and economic status', *Employment Gazette*, December.

Baron, H.M. (1975) 'Racial domination in advanced capitalism: a theory of nationalism and divisions in the labour market', in R.C. Edwards, M. Reich and D.M. Gordon (eds) *Labor Market Segmentation*, Lexington, Mass.: D.C. Heath.

Barron, R.D. and Norris, G.M. (1976) 'Sexual divisions and the dual labour market', in D.L. Barker and S. Allen (eds) *Dependence and Exploitation in Work and Marriage*, London: Longman.

Becker, G.S. (1957) *The Economics of Discrimination*, Chicago: University of Chicago Press.

Becker, G.S. (1962) 'Investment in human capital', *Journal of Political Economy*, vol. 70.

Becker, G.S. (1975) *Human Capital: a theoretical and empirical analysis*, New York: National Bureau of Economic Research.

Becker, G.S. (1976) *The Economic Approach to Human Behavior*, Chicago: University of Chicago Press.

Beechey, V. (1978) 'Women and production: a critical analysis of some sociological theories of women's work', in A. Kuhn and A. Wolpe (eds) *Feminism and Materialism*, London: Routledge.

Beechey, V. (1986) 'Women and employment in contemporary Britain', in V. Beechey and E. Whitelegg (eds) *Women in Britain Today*, Milton Keynes: Open University Press.

Beechey, V. (1987) *Unequal Work*, London: Verso.

Berg, I. (with the assistance of Gorelick, S.) (1971) *Education and Jobs: the great training robbery*, Boston: Beacon Press.

Berg, I. (ed.) (1981) *Sociological Perspectives on Labour Markets*, New York: Academic Press.

Berg, M. (1987) 'Women's work, mechanisation and the early phases of industrialisation in England' in P. Joyce (ed) *The Historical Meanings of Work*, Cambridge: Cambridge University Press.

Berger, J. and Mohr, J. (1975) *A Seventh Man*, Harmondsworth: Penguin.

Beveridge, W. (1944) *Full Employment in a Free Society*, London: George Allen and Unwin.

Blackburn, R.M. and Mann, M. (1979) *The Working Class in the Labour Market*, London: Macmillan.

Blau, P. and Duncan, O.D. (1969) *The American Occupational Structure*, New York: John Wiley.

Blauner, R. (1972) *Racial Oppression in America*, New York: Harper and Row.

Bluestone, B. and Stevenson, M.H. (1981) 'Industrial transformation and the evolution of dual labour markets: the case of the retail trade in the United States', in F. Wilkinson (ed.) *The Dynamics of Labour Market Segmentation*, London: Academic Press.

Böhning, W.R. (1972) *The Migration of Workers in the U.K. and the European Community*, Oxford: Oxford University Press for the Institute of Race Relations.

Bonacich, E. (1972) 'A theory of ethnic antagonism: the split labor market', *American Sociological Review*, vol. 37, pp. 547–59.

Bonacich, E. (1976) 'Advanced capitalism and black/white race relations in the United States: a split labor market interpretation', *American Sociological Review*, vol. 41, pp. 34–51.

Bowles, S. and Gintis, H. (1976) *Schooling in Capitalist America*, London: Routledge and Kegan Paul.

Bradley, H. (1989) *Men's Work, Women's Work*, Cambridge: Polity Press.

Bradley, H. (1990) 'Change and continuity in history and sociology: the case of industrial paternalism', in S. Kendrick, P. Straw and D. McCrone (eds) *Interpreting the Past, Understanding the Present*, Basingstoke: Macmillan.

Braverman, H. (1974) *Labor and Monopoly Capital – the degradation of work in the twentieth century*, New York: Monthly Review Press.

Bresnen, M., Wray, K., Bryman, A., Beardsworth, A.D., Ford, J.R. and Keil, E.T. (1985) 'The flexibility of recruitment in the construction industry: formalisation or re-casualisation?', *Sociology*, vol. 19, no. 1, pp. 108–24.

Brooks, D. (1975) *Race and Labour in London Transport*, Oxford: Oxford University Press for the Institute of Race Relations.

Brown, C. (1984) *Black and White Britain: the third PSI study*, London: Heinemann.

Brown, P. (1987) *Schooling Ordinary Kids*, London: Tavistock.

Brown, R.K. (1982) 'Work histories, career strategies and the class structure', in A. Giddens and G. Mackenzie (eds) *Social Class and the Division of Labour*, Cambridge: Cambridge University Press.

Burawoy, M. (1979) *Manufacturing Consent*, Chicago: University of Chicago Press.

Burawoy, M. and Lukács, J. (1989) 'What is socialist about socialist production? Autonomy and control in a Hungarian steel mill', in S. Wood (ed.) *The Transformation of Work?*, London: Unwin Hyman.

Byrne, E. (1978) *Women and Education*, London: Tavistock.

Bythell, D. (1969) *The Handloom Weavers*, Cambridge: Cambridge University Press.

Bythell, D. (1978) *The Sweated Trades: outwork in nineteenth century Britain*, London: Batsford.

Canning, D. (1984) 'A theory of wages and employment' in *Internal, Local and Regional Labour Markets*, Cambridge: Department of Applied Economics, University of Cambridge.

Carmichael, S. and Hamilton, C.C. (1968) *Black Power: the politics of liberation in America*, London: Jonathan Cape.

Castles, S. and Kosack, G. (1973) *Immigrant Workers and Class Structure in Western Europe*, Oxford: Oxford University Press for the Institute of Race Relations.

Catt, H. (1984) 'Recruiting manual workers in high unemployment: an employer's experience', *Industrial Relations Journal*, 15, pp. 90–3.

Cicourel, A.V. (1968) *The Social Organisation of Juvenile Justice*, New York: Wiley.

Cockburn, C. (1983) *Brothers; male dominance and technological change*, London: Pluto Press.

Cohen, R. (1987) *The New Helots: migrants in the international division of labour*, Aldershot: Gower.

Cornfield, D.B. (1981) 'Industrial social organization and layoffs in American manufacturing industry', in I. Berg (ed.) *Sociological Perspectives on Labor Markets*, New York: Academic Press.

Cornfield, D.B. (1987) 'Ethnic inequality in layoff chances: the impact of unionisation on layoff procedure', in R.M. Lee (ed.) *Redundancy, Layoffs and Plant Closures*, London: Croom Helm.

Corrigan, P.R.D.C. (1977) 'Feudal relics or capitalist monuments? notes on the sociology of unfree labour', *Sociology*, vol. 11, no. 3, pp. 435–63.

Coxon, A. and Jones, C. (1978) *The Images of Occupational Prestige*, London: Macmillan.

Coxon, A. and Jones, C. (1979) *Class and Hierarchy: the social meaning of occupations*, London: Macmillan.

Coyle, A. (1982) 'Sex and skill in the organisation of the clothing industry', in J. West (ed.) *Work, Women and the Labour Market*, London: Routledge Kegan Paul.

Craig, C., Rubery, J., Tarling, R. and Wilkinson, F. (1982) *Labour Market Structure, Industrial Organisation and Low Pay*, Cambridge: Cambridge University Press.

Craig, C., Rubery, J., Tarling, R. and Wilkinson, F. (1985) 'Economic, social and political factors in the operation of the labour market', in B. Roberts, R. Finnegan and D. Gallie (eds) *New Approaches to Economic Life*, Manchester: Manchester University Press.

Crompton, R. and Jones, G. (1984) *White-collar Proletariat*, London: Macmillan.

Crompton, R. and Sanderson, K. (1990) *Gendered Jobs and Social Change*, London: Unwin Hyman.

Crow, G. (1989) 'The use of the concept of "strategy" in recent sociological literature', *Sociology*, vol. 23, no. 1, pp. 1–24.

Curran, M.M. (1988) 'Gender and recruitment: people and places in the labour market', *Work, Employment and Society*, vol. 2, no. 2, pp. 335–51.

Danson, M. (1982) 'The industrial structure and labour market segmentation: urban and regional implications', *Regional Studies*, vol. 16, no. 4.

Danson, M. (ed.) (1986) *Redundancy and Recession: restructuring the regions?*, Norwich: Geo Books.

Davis, J. (1985) 'Rules not laws: an ethnographic approach to economics', in B. Roberts, R. Finnegan and D. Gallie (eds) *New Approaches to Economic Life*, Manchester: Manchester University Press.

Davis, K. and Moore, W.E. (1945) 'Some principles of stratification', *American Sociological Review*, vol. 10, pp. 242–9.

De Grazia, R. (1984) *Clandestine Employment*, Geneva: International Labour Organisation.

Deem, R. (ed.) (1980) *Schooling for Women's Work*, London: Routledge and Kegan Paul.

Delphy, C. (1977) *The Main Enemy: a materialist analysis of women's oppression*, Explorations in Feminism No. 3, London: Women's Research and Resources Centre.

Dex, S. (1985) *The Sexual Division of Work*, Brighton: Wheatsheaf.

Dex, S. (1987) *Women's Occupational Mobility: a lifetime perspective*, Basingstoke: Macmillan.

Dex, S. (1988) *Women's Attitudes Towards Work*, Basingstoke: Macmillan.

DiPrete, T.A. and Grusky, D.B. (1990) 'Structure and trend in the process of stratification for American men and women', *American Journal of Sociology*, vol. 96, no. 1, pp. 107–43.

Doeringer, P.B. (1986) 'Internal labor markets and noncompeting groups', *American Economic Review*, Papers and Proceedings, vol. 76, pp. 48–52.

Doeringer, P.B. and Piore, M.J. (1971) *Internal Labor Markets and Manpower Analysis*, Lexington: D.C. Heath.

Driver, C. (1970) *Tory Radical: the life of Richard Oastler*, New York: Octagon Books.

Durkheim, E. (1933) *The Division of Labour in Society*, New York: Macmillan.

Dworkin, R. (1980) 'Reverse discrimination' in P. Braham, E. Rhodes and

M. Pearn (eds) *Discrimination and Disadvantage in Employment*, London: Harper and Row.

Edwards, R.C. (1979) *Contested Terrain: the transformation of the workplace in the twentieth century*, London: Heinemann.

Elster, J. (1985) *Making Sense of Marx*, Cambridge: Cambridge University Press.

Equal Opportunities Commission (1986) 'Methodological issues in gender research', *Research Bulletin*, no. 10 (Autumn).

Fallon, P. and Verry, D. (1988) *The Economics of Labour Markets*, Hemel Hempstead: Philip Allan.

Fevre, R. (1984) *Cheap Labour and Racial Discrimination*, Aldershot: Gower.

Fevre, R. (1985) 'Racial discrimination and competition in British trade unions', *Ethnic and Racial Studies*, vol. 8, no. 4, pp. 563–80.

Fevre, R. (1987) 'Redundancy and the labour market: the role of "readaption benefits"', in R.M. Lee (ed.) *Redundancy, Layoffs and Plant Closures*, London: Croom Helm.

Fevre, R. (1989a) 'Informal practices, flexible firms and private labour markets', *Sociology*, vol. 23, no. 1, pp. 91–109.

Fevre, R. (1989b) *Wales is Closed*, Nottingham: Spokesman Books.

Fevre, R. (1991) 'The growth of alternatives to full-time and permanent employment in the United Kingdom', in P. Brown and R. Scase (eds) *Poor Work: disadvantage and the division of labour*, Milton Keynes: Open University Press.

Foucault, M. (1970) *The Order of Things*, London: Tavistock.

Freedman, M. (1976) *Labor Markets: segments and shelters*, Montclair: Allanheld Osmun and Co.

Friedman, A. (1978) *Industry and Labour*, Basingstoke: Macmillan.

Fröbel, F., Heinrichs, J. and Kreye, D. (1980) *The New International Division of Labour – structural unemployment in industrialised countries and industrialisation in developing countries*, Cambridge: Cambridge University Press – Editions de la Maison des Sciences de l'homme, Paris.

Fryer, P. (1984) *Staying Power: the history of black people in Britain*, London: Pluto Press.

Fulcher, J. (1987) 'Labour movement theory versus corporatism: social democracy in Sweden', *Sociology*, vol. 21, no. 2, pp. 231–52.

Fyfe, A. (1989) *Child Labour*, Cambridge: Polity Press.

Game, R. and Pringle, R. (1983) *Gender at Work*, London: Allen and Unwin.

Garnsey, E. (1982) 'Women's work and theories of class and stratification', in A. Giddens and D. Held (eds) *Classes, Power and Conflict*, London: Macmillan.

Garnsey, E., Rubery, J. and Wilkinson, F. (1985) 'Labour market structure and work-force divisions', in R. Deem and G. Salaman (eds) *Work, Culture and Society*, Milton Keynes: Open University Press.

Gensior, S. and Schöler, B. (1989) 'Women's employment and multinationals in the Federal Republic of Germany', in D. Elson and R. Pearson (eds) *Women's Employment and Multi-nationals in Europe*, London: Macmillan.

Giddens, A. (1981) *The Class Structure of the Advanced Societies*, second edition, London: Hutchinson.

Giddens, A. (1984) *The Constitution of Society: outline of the theory of structuration*, Cambridge: Polity Press.

Glazer, N. (1980) 'From equal opportunity to statistical parity', in P. Braham, E. Rhodes and M. Pearn (eds) *Discrimination and Disadvantage in Employment*, London: Harper and Row.

Goldthorpe, J.H. (1982) 'On the service class, its formation and future', in A. Giddens and G. Mackenzie (eds) *Social Class and the Division of Labour*, Cambridge: Cambridge University Press.

Goldthorpe, J.H. (1984) 'The end of convergence: corporatist and dualist tendencies in modern western societies' in J.H. Goldthorpe (ed.) *Order and Conflict in Contemporary Capitalism*, Oxford: Oxford University Press.

Goldthorpe, J.H. (with Llewellyn, C. and Payne, C.) (1987) *Social Mobility and Class Structure in Modern Britain*, Oxford: Clarendon Press.

Goldthorpe, J.H., Lockwood, D., Bechofer, F. and Platt, J. (1968) *The Affluent Worker: industrial attitudes and behaviour*, Cambridge: Cambridge University Press.

Goldthorpe, J.H. and Payne, C. (1986) 'Trends in intergenerational class mobility in England and Wales 1972–83', *Sociology*, vol. 20, no. 1, pp. 1–24.

Gordon, D.M. (1972) *Theories of Poverty and Unemployment*, Lexington: D.C. Heath.

Granovetter, M. (1973) 'The strength of weak ties', *American Journal of Sociology*, vol. 78, pp. 1360–80.

Granovetter, M. (1974) *Getting a Job: a study of contacts and careers*, Cambridge, Mass.: Harvard University Press.

Granovetter, M. (1981) 'Towards a sociological theory of income differences', in I. Berg (ed.) *Sociological Perspectives on Labour Markets*, London: Academic Press.

Grieco, M. (1987) *Keeping it in the Family; social networks and employment chance*, London: Tavistock.

Halsey, A.H. (1981) *Change in British Society*, Milton Keynes: Open University Press.

Halsey, A.H., Heath, A.F. and Ridge, J.M. (1980) *Origins and Destinations*, Oxford: Clarendon Press.

Harris, C.C. (1984) *The Idea of a Labour Market*, School of Social Studies Occasional Paper no. 4, Swansea: University College of Swansea.

Harris, C.C. and Lee, R.M. (1988) 'Conceptualizing the place of redundant steelworkers in the class structure', in D. Rose (ed.) *Social Stratification and Economic Change*, London: Hutchinson.

Harris, C.C. and the Redundancy and Unemployment Research Group (1987) *Redundancy and Recession*, Oxford: Basil Blackwell.

Hartman, H. (1979) 'The unhappy marriage of Marxism and feminism: towards a more progressive union', *Capital and Class*, no. 8, pp. 1–33.

Hauser, R.M. and Featherman, D.L. (1977) *The Process of Stratification*, New York: Academic Press.

Heath, A. (1976) *Rational Choice and Social Exchange: a critique of exchange theory*, Cambridge: Cambridge University Press.

Hechter, M. (ed.) (1983) *The Microfoundations of Macrosociology*, Philadelphia: Temple University Press.

Hobsbawm, E.J. (1964) *Labouring Men*, London: Weidenfeld and Nicolson.

Hodgson, G. (1988) *Economics and Institutions*, Cambridge: Polity Press.

Hudson, R. and Sadler, D. (1989) *The International Steel Industry: restructuring state policies and localities*, London: Routledge.

Hyman, R. (1987) 'Strategy or structure? capital, labour and control', *Work, Employment and Society*, vol. 1, no. 1, pp. 25–35.

Illich, I. (1971) *Deschooling Society*, Harmondsworth: Penguin.

Jackson, P. and Barry, U. (1989) 'Women's employment and multinationals in the Republic of Ireland' in D. Elson and R. Pearson (eds) *Women's Employment and Multi–nationals in Europe*, London: Macmillan.

Jencks, C., Smith, M., Acland, H., Bane, M.J., Cohen, D., Gintis, H., Heyns, B. and Michelson, S. (1972) *Inequality*, New York: Basic Books.

Jenkins, R. (1983) *Lads, Citizens and Ordinary Kids*, London: Routledge Kegan Paul.

Jenkins, R. (1984) 'Acceptability, suitability and the search for the habituated worker: how ethnic minorities and women lose out', *International Journal of Social Economics*, vol. 11, no. 7, pp. 65–75.

Jenkins, R. (1986) *Racism and Recruitment*, Cambridge: Cambridge University Press.

Jenkins, R. (1988) 'Discrimination and equal opportunity in employment: ethnicity and "race" in the United Kingdom', in D. Gallie (ed.) *Employment in Britain*, Oxford: Basil Blackwell.

Jenkins, R., Bryman, A., Ford, J., Keil, T. and Beardsworth, A. (1983) 'Information in the labour market: the impact of the recession', *Sociology*, vol. 17, pp. 260–7.

Jewson, N. and Mason, D. (1986) 'Modes of discrimination in the recruitment process: formalisation, fairness and efficiency', *Sociology*, vol. 20, no. 1, pp. 43–63.

Joll, C., Mckenna, C., McNabb, R. and Shorey, J. (1983) *Developments in Labour Market Analysis*, London: George Allen and Unwin.

Jordan, B. (1982) *Mass Unemployment and the Future of Britain*, Oxford: Basil Blackwell.

Kaufman, R.L. (1986) 'The impact of industrial and occupational structure on black–white employment allocation', *American Sociological Review*, vol. 51, pp. 310–23.

Keane, J. and Owens, J. (1986) *After Full Employment*, London: Hutchinson.

Kertesi, G. and Sziráczki, G. (1988) 'Worker behaviour in the labour market', in R.E. Pahl (ed.) *On Work*, Oxford: Basil Blackwell.

Keyssar, A. (1986) *Out of Work: the first century of unemployment in Massachusetts*, Cambridge: Cambridge University Press.

Kornai, J. (1980) *The Economics of Shortage*, Amsterdam: North Holland Publishing Company.

Kreckel, R. (1980) 'Unequal opportunity structure and labour market segmentation', *Sociology*, vol. 14, pp. 525–50.

Kuhn, S. (1989) 'The limits to industrialization: computer software development in a large commercial bank', in S. Wood (ed.) *The Transformation of Work?*, London: Unwin Hyman.

Kumazawa, M. and Yamada, J. (1989) 'Jobs and skills under the lifelong nenkō employment practice', in S. Wood (ed.) *The Transformation of Work?*, London: Unwin Hyman.

Labour and Society (1987), vol. 12, no. 1.

Land, H. (1980) 'The family wage', *Feminist Review*, (6).

Lane, C. (1987) 'The impact of the economic and political system on social stratification and social mobility: Soviet lower white-collar workers in comparative perspective', *Sociology*, vol. 21, no. 2, pp. 171–98.

Lazonick, W. (1978) 'Industrial relations and technical change: the case of the self–acting mule', *Cambridge Journal of Economics*, vol. 3, pp. 231–62.

Leadbeater, C. and Lloyd, J. (1986) *In Search of Work*, Harmondsworth: Penguin.

Lee, D. (1989) 'The transformation of training and the transformation of work in Britain', in S. Wood (ed.) *The Transformation of Work?*, London: Unwin Hyman.

Lindbeck, A. and Snower, D.J. (1987) *Cooperation, Harassment, and Involuntary Unemployment: an insider-outsider approach*, C.E.P.R. Discussion Paper no. 196, London: Centre for Economic Policy Research.

Lockwood, D. (1958) *The Blackcoated Worker*, London: George Allen and Unwin.

MacInnes, J. (1987) *Thatcherism at Work; industrial relations and economic change*, Milton Keynes: Open University Press.

Mackay, R. (1988) Review of C.C. Harris and the Redundancy and Unemployment Research Group, *Redundancy and Recession*, *Economic Journal*, vol. 98, p. 601.

McRae, S. and Daniel, W.W. (1991) *Maternity Rights*, London: Policy Studies Institute.

Maguire, M. (1986) 'Recruitment as a means of control', in K. Purcell, S. Wood, A. Waton and S. Allen (eds) *The Changing Experience of Employment*, Basingstoke: Macmillan.

Manwaring, T. (1984) 'The extended internal labour market', *Cambridge Journal of Economics*, vol. 8, pp. 161–87.

Marsden, D. (1986) *The End of Economic Man? custom and competition in labour markets*, Brighton: Wheatsheaf.

Marshall, R. (1974) 'The economics of racial discrimination: a survey', *Journal of Economic Literature*, vol. 12, no. 3, pp. 849–71.

Martin, R. and Fryer, R. (1973) *Redundancy and Paternalist Capitalism*, London: Allen and Unwin.

Martin, R. and Rowthorn, B. (1986) *The Geography of Deindustrialisation*, London: Macmillan.

Marx, K. (1976) *Capital*, Volume One, Harmondsworth: Penguin.

Massey, D. and Meagan, R. (1982) *The Anatomy of Job Loss: the how, why and where of employment decline*, London: Methuen.

Maurice, M., Sellier, F. and Silvestre, J. (1986) *The Social Foundations of Industrial Power*, Cambridge, Mass.: MIT Press.

Melossi, D. and Pavarini, M. (1981) *The Prison and the Factory: origins of the penitentiary system*, London: Macmillan.

Miles, R. (1987) *Capitalism and Unfree Labour – anomaly or necessity?*, London: Tavistock.

Miles, R. (1989) *Racism*, London: Routledge.

Miles, R. (1990) 'Whatever happened to the sociology of migration?', *Work, Employment and Society*, vol. 4, no. 2, pp. 281–98.

Miller, R.K. (1981) 'Patterns of employment difficulty among European immigrant industrial workers during the Great Depression: local opportunity and cultural heritage', in I. Berg (ed.) *Sociological Perspectives on Labor Markets*, New York: Academic Press.

Millett, K. (1977) *Sexual Politics*, London: Virago.

Mills, C.W. (1959) *The Sociological Imagination*, Oxford: Oxford University Press.

Minford, P. (1985) *Unemployment – Cause and Cure*, Oxford: Basil Blackwell.

Minford, P. and Peel, D. (1981) 'Is the government's economic strategy on course?', *Lloyds Bank Review*, no. 140 (April), pp. 1–19.

Morris, C.N. and Dilnot, A.W. (1982) *The Effects of the Tax and Benefit System on the Employment Decision*, London: Institute of Fiscal Studies.

Moynihan, D.P. (1969) *On Understanding Poverty: Perspectives from the Social Sciences*, New York: Basic Books.

Neumann, L. (1989) 'Market relations in intra-enterprise wage bargaining?', *Acta Oeconomica*, vol. 40, no. 1, pp. 69–86.

Nichols, T. and Beynon, H. (1977) *Living with Capitalism*, London: Routledge and Kegan Paul.

Norris, G.M. (1978a) 'Unemployment, subemployment and personal characteristics: (a) the inadequacies of traditional approaches to unemployment', *Sociological Review*, vol. 26, no. 1, pp. 89–108.

Norris, G.M. (1978b) 'Unemployment, subemployment and personal characteristics: (b) job separation and work histories', *Sociological Review*, vol. 26, no. 2, pp. 327–47.

Norris, G.M. (1978c) 'Industrial paternalist capitalism and local labour markets', *Sociology*, vol. 12, no. 3, pp. 469–89.

O'Dowd, L., Rolston, B. and Tomlinson, M. (1980) *Northern Ireland: between civil rights and civil war*, London: C.S.E.

Offe, C. (1985) *Disorganized Capitalism*, Oxford: Polity Press.

Office of Population Censuses and Surveys (OPCS) (1987) *Labour Force Survey 1985*, London: H.M.S.O.

Office of Population Censuses and Surveys (OPCS) (1989a) *Labour Force Survey 1987*, London: H.M.S.O.

Office of Population Censuses and Surveys (OPCS) (1989b) *General Household Survey 1987*, London: H.M.S.O.

Parkin, F. (1979) *Marxism and Class Theory – a bourgeois critique*, London: Tavistock.

Parsons, T. (1951) *The Social System*, New York: Free Press.

Parsons, T. 'Introduction' to Weber M. (1964) *The Theory of Social and Economic Organisation*, New York: Free Press.

Parsons, T. and Shils, E. (1951) *Towards a General Theory of Social Action*, Cambridge, Mass.: Harvard University Press.

Phillips, A. and Taylor, B. (1980) 'Sex and Skill: notes towards a feminist economics', *Feminist Review*, 6, pp. 79–88.

Pinchbeck, I. (1981) *Women Workers and the Industrial Revolution*, London: Virago.

Piore, M.J. (1980) *Birds of Passage – migrant labour and industrial societies*, Cambridge: Cambridge University Press.

Piore, M.J. (1987) 'Historical perspectives and the interpretation of unemployment', *Journal of Economic Literature*, vol. 25, pp. 1834–50.

Piore, M.J. and Sabel, C.F. (1984) *The Second Industrial Divide – possibilities for prosperity*, New York: Basic Books.

Polanyi, K. (1957) 'The economy as instituted process', in K. Polanyi, C.M. Arensberg and H.W. Pearson *Trade and Market in the Early Empires*, Glencoe: Free Press.

Pollert, A. (1987) *The 'Flexible Firm': a model in search of reality (or a policy in search of a practice?)*, Warwick Papers in Industrial Relations no. 19, University of Warwick: Industrial Relations Research Unit.

Purdy, D.L. (1988) *Social Power and the Labour Market*, Basingstoke: Macmillan.

Rainnie, A. (1989) *Industrial Relations in Small Firms: small isn't beautiful*, London: Routledge.

Rattansi, A. (1981) *Marx and the Division of Labour*, London: Macmillan.

Rattansi, A. (1982) 'Marx and the abolition of the division of labour' in A. Giddens and G. Mackenzie (eds) *Social Class and the Division of Labour*, Cambridge: Cambridge University Press.

Redford, A. (1926) *Labour Migration in England 1800–1850*, Manchester: Manchester University Press.

Rex, J. and Moore, R. (1967) *Race, Community and Conflict*, Oxford: Oxford University Press.

Reynolds, L.G. (1951) *The Structure of Labor Markets*, New York: Harper and Brothers.

Rich, P. (1986) *Race and Empire in British Politics*, Cambridge: Cambridge University Press.

Roberts, K. (1975) 'The developmental theory of occupational choice: a critique and an alternative', in G. Esland, G. Salaman and M. Speakman (eds) *People and Work*, Edinburgh: Holmes Macdougall.

Roberts, K., Noble, M. and Duggan, J. (1984) 'Youth unemployment: an old problem or a new lifestyle?' in K. Thompson (ed.) *Work, Employment and Unemployment*, Milton Keynes: Open University Press.

Rose, M. (1988) *Industrial Behaviour*, (Second Edition) Harmondsworth: Penguin.

Rosenbaum, J.E. and Kariya, T. (1989) 'From high school to work: market and institutional mechanisms in Japan', *American Journal of Sociology*, vol. 94, no. 6, pp. 1334–65.

Rubery, J. (1978) 'Structured labour markets, worker organisation and low pay', *Cambridge Journal of Economics*, vol. 2, no. 1, pp. 17–36.

Rueschemeyer, D. (1986) *Power and the Division of Labour*, Cambridge: Polity Press.

Sabel, C.F. (1982) *Work and Politics – the division of labour in industry*, Cambridge: Cambridge University Press.

Salais, R., Bavarez, N. and Reynaud, B. (1986) *L'invention du Chômage: histoire et transformations d'une catégorie en France des années 1890 aux années 1980*, Paris: Presses Universitaires de France.

Sapsford, D. (1981) *Labour Economics*, London: George Allen and Unwin.

Scase, R. and Goffee, R. (1989) *Reluctant Managers: their work and lifestyles*, London: Unwin Hyman.

Schervish, P.G. (1981) 'The structure of employment and unemployment', in I. Berg (ed.) *Sociological Perspectives on Labor Markets*, New York: Academic Press.

Schervish, P.G. (1983) *The Structural Determinants of Unemployment*, New York: Academic Press.

Sewell, W. and Hauser, R.M. (1975) *Education, Occupation and Earnings*, New York: Academic Press.

Sivanandan, A. (1982) *A Different Hunger: writings on black resistance*, London: Pluto Press.

Smelser, N.J. (1959) *Social Change in the Industrial Revolution*, Chicago: University of Chicago Press.

Smelser, N.J. (1963) *The Sociology of Economic Life*, Englewood Cliffs, New Jersey: Prentice Hall.

Social Trends (1989), London: H.M.S.O.

Sørensen, A.B. and Kalleberg, A.L. (1981) 'An outline of a theory of the matching of persons to jobs' in I. Berg (ed.) *Sociological Perspectives on Labor Markets*, New York: Academic Press.

Sowell, T. (1981a) *Markets and Minorities*, Oxford: Basil Blackwell for the International Center for Economic Policy Studies.

Sowell, T. (1981b) *Ethnic America: a history*, New York: Basic Books.

Stark, D. (1986) 'Rethinking internal labor markets: new insights from a comparative perspective', *American Sociological Review*, vol. 51, pp. 492–504.

Stewart, A., Prandy, K. and Blackburn, R.M. (1980) *Social Stratification and Occupations*, London: Macmillan.

Stewart, A., Blackburn, R.M. and Prandy, K. (1985) 'Gender and earnings: the failure of market explanations', in B. Roberts, R. Finnegan and D. Gallie (eds) *New Approaches to Economic Life*, Manchester: Manchester University Press.

Therborn, G. (1985) *Why Some Peoples are More Unemployed than Others*, London: Verso.

Thompson, E.P. (1967) 'Time, work-discipline and industrial capitalism', *Past and Present*, no. 38, pp. 56–97.

Thompson, E.P. (1974) *The Making of the English Working Class*, Harmondsworth: Penguin.

Thurrow, L. (1975) *Generating Inequality: mechanisms of distribution in the U.S. economy*, New York: Basic Books.

Tumin, M.M. (1967) *Social Stratification – the forms and functions of inequality*, Englewood Cliffs, New Jersey: Prentice Hall.

Walby, S. (1986) *Patriarchy at Work: patriarchal and capitalist relations in employment*, Cambridge: Polity Press.

Walby, S. (ed.) (1988) *Gender Segregation at Work*, Milton Keynes: Open University Press.

Wallace, M. and Kalleberg, A.L. (1981) 'Economic organization of firms and labour market consequences: toward a specification of dual economy theory', in I. Berg (ed.) *Sociological Perspectives on Labor Markets*, New York: Academic Press.

Weber, M. (1930) *The Protestant Ethic and the Spirit of Capitalism*, London: Unwin University Books.

Weber, M. (1948) 'Class, status and party', in *From Max Weber: essays in sociology*, Oxford: Oxford University Press, pp. 180–95.

Weber, M. (1949) *The Methodology of the Social Sciences*, New York: Free Press.

Weber, M. (1964) *The Theory of Social and Economic Organization*, New York: Free Press.

Weber, M. (1968) *Economy and Society*, G. Roth and C. Wittich (eds), New York: Bedminster Press.

Williams, W.M. (ed.) (1974) *Occupational Choice*, London: George Allen and Unwin.

Williamson, O.E. (1975) *Markets and Hierarchies: analysis and antitrust implications*, New York: Free Press.

Willis, P. (1977) *Learning to Labour*, Farnborough: Saxon House.

Windolf, P. and Wood, S. (1988) *Recruitment and Selection in the Labour Market*, Aldershot: Gower.

Wing, C. (1967) *The Evils of the Factory System*, London: Frank Cass.

INDEX OF PROPER NAMES

INDEX OF SUBJECTS

severance pay, 104, 162
shift work, 141
'shortage economies', 127, 128
short-time working, 142
signs, 65, 66, 67, 75
skilled work, workers, 5, 33, 34, 66,
  97, 100, 103, 104
skills, 4, 5, 17, 32, 56, 64, 66, 71, 75,
  99–101, 107, 108, 116n, 143–4,
  146
  non-transferable, 100–1
  tacit, 108–9, 144, 146
  transferable, 32, 100–1
slavery, 120, 121
social
  background, 70
  change, 18, 21, 41, 42, 49
  closure, 57–8, 94, 155, 161
  construction, 52, 60, 80, 113, 156–7,
    159, 166–9, 170n
  division, 43
  groups, 42, 43, 44, 53–8, 76, 83–96,
    98, 99, 109, 113, 114, 116n,
    118, 122, 129, 130, 154–5, 165,
    166, 169, 170n
  hierarchy, 47, 51–2, 53, 54, 58–68,
    70, 76, 81n, 86, 96, 97, 129,
    152–3, 155, 170n
  identities, 43
  institutions 53–8, 76, 83–96, 98, 99,
    113, 118, 129, 130, 155, 165,
    169
  interaction, 42, 43, 44, 154, 156,
    158, 161
  mobility, 40, 54, 56, 70, 73, 107,
    142
  networks, 57, 70, 71, 109
  problems, 136, 137
  relations, 42, 43, 44, 45, 53–8, 76,
    83–96, 98, 99, 113, 118, 122,
    129, 130, 154–5, 165, 169
  science, 19, 23, 41, 44, 120, 139,
    157
  stratification, 60, 62, 64, 81n
  values, 52, 58–68, 70, 76, 80, 96,
    114, 167, 169
    market values, 59, 64–8, 71, 74–5,
      78–9, 96, 97, 114, 115, 153–4,
      160–2, 166
    people values, 59–62, 70, 71, 72,
      76, 77, 78–9, 80, 96, 97, 114,
      115, 153–4, 160, 161–2, 166,
      170n

work values, 59, 62–4, 71–4, 76,
  77, 79, 80, 96, 97, 114, 115,
  117n, 153–4, 160–2, 166, 170n
social anthropology, 169
Social Charter, 131, 142
Social and Economic Life Initiative, 20,
  168
social workers, 121, 163
socialism, 128
society, 42–3, 45, 49, 53, 60, 62, 75,
  96, 118–19, 122, 136, 148, 164,
  169
sociology, 13, 18–21, 23, 30, 37, 38,
  47, 49, 52, 53, 55, 56, 59, 72,
  74, 75, 76, 78, 81n, 83, 85, 86,
  93, 96, 98, 99, 108, 115, 116n,
  118, 130, 134, 137, 143, 168–9
  economic, 19–21, 169
  of labour markets, 10, 11, 12, 13,
    21, 22n, 24, 38–45, 58, 84, 97,
    105, 106, 114, 118, 119, 129,
    129, 148, 149n, 151–2, 155–68
  of migration, 148
  of work, 12, 24
South Africa, 6, 44, 140
Soviet Union, 142
specialisation, 49, 50, 51, 94, 116n,
  152
  and cooperation, 85–9, 96, 98, 113,
    155
stages of the life-cycle, 61, 70
starvation, 94
state, 40, 43, 44, 58, 90, 92, 118–50,
  155, 157, 165
  certification, 146
  decentralised, 123, 124
  intervention, 6, 7, 8, 137–8
  licensing, 145–6
statistics, 15–18, 41, 66
status, 17, 54
status attainment theory, 53–4, 155
steelworkers, 15–16
strategy, 32, 92, 106–7, 110, 111
structural change, 68, 102
'structural differentiation', 86, 116n
structural-functionalism, 62–4, 65, 67,
  87–9, 94
students, 145
subcultures, 54
subsistence, 90, 94
suitability, 108–9
surplus value, 91, 116n
Sweden, 6, 123, 142

———